YORK
in the 1960s

Ten Years That Changed a City

PAUL CHRYSTAL

AMBERLEY

Beware how you destroy your antiquities, guard them with religious care! They are what give you a decided character and superiority over other provincial cities. You have lost much, take care of what remains.

William Etty (1787–1849)

First published 2015

Amberley Publishing
The Hill, Stroud
Gloucestershire, GL5 4EP

www.amberley-books.com

British Library Cataloguing in Publication Data.
A catalogue record for this book is available from the British Library.

ISBN 978 1 4456 4063 1 (print)
ISBN 978 1 4456 4096 9 (ebook)

Typesetting and Origination by Amberley Publishing.
Printed in the UK.

Contents

About the Author

Paul Chrystal was educated at the universities of Hull and Southampton where he took degrees in classics. He has worked in medical publishing for thirty-five years but now combines this with advising local visitor attractions such as the National Trust in York and York's Chocolate Story, writing features for national newspapers, as well as appearing regularly on BBC radio and on the BBC World Service. He is the author of forty or so books published since 2010 on a wide range of subjects including classical history and social histories of chocolate, coffee and tea. His many books on York include *The Rowntree Family*, *A History of Chocolate in York*, *York Industries*, *Confectionery in Yorkshire*, *Secret York*, *A-Z of York* and *York in the 1950s*. *York in the 1970s* is in press, due for publication in 2016. Paul is married with three children and lives near York.

Introduction

This is the second volume in a unique, exciting and revealing new series on the history of York, the first of which, *York in the 1950s*, has already been published. Until this series, none of the many books published on the extensive and exhilarating history and heritage of York focused on what was happening here in one particular decade. *York in the 1960s: Ten Years That Changed a City* provides a uniquely focussed account of York life in the 1960s – ten years in which the city emerged from the greyness of the largely derelict 1950s into a technicolour world of increasing personal freedom and growing disposable incomes allowing some to spend that money on labour-saving white goods, ubiquitous cars and on foreign food and holidays, in supermarkets and voguish department stores and in record shops. Innovative popular music was top of the pops while art and theatre persistently pushed back the boundaries. As with the '50s, but even more so, much of what we now see, enjoy and cherish in York owes its origins to work worked and plans planned in the 1960s.

Specific to York in the '60s was the ground-breaking Esher Report and the long overdue establishment of the University of York. The former, despite initially a degree of reluctance, naivety and exclusiveness on the part of the local council, was of prodigious importance to the city, literally paving the way for the preservation and conservation of much of what we can still see and enjoy in York today, one of Europe's finest cities. The happy balance of an historic yet functional city is due in large part to Lord Esher, with not a little help from some friends in the shape of York Civic Trust, the Georgian Society and YAYAS. The university was a long time coming but its social, cultural, educational and scientific importance to the city was, and remains, inestimable.

York in the 1960s explores all of these aspects of York, and much, much more, in that energetic decade of dynamism and revitalisation. It will have appeal, give pleasure and satisfy curiosity whether you grew up here then, whether you have left and want to rekindle your childhood and teenage memories, or whether you are just a child of the 1960s and are curious to know what happened and what was going on here then. *York in the 1960s* will entertain, fascinate and inform with its facts, rarely seen photographs and its sheer, unadulterated nostalgia.

Paul Chrystal, York, September 2015

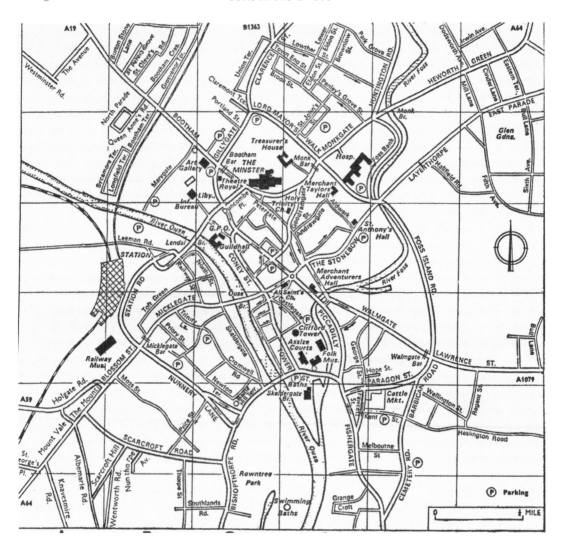

Chapter 1

1960s Britain

Britain in the 1950s exuded an overriding greyness, occasionally alleviated by glimpses of optimism and technicolour, notably the wedding of Queen Elizabeth II and the Festival of Britain. There were signs too of an end to post-war austerity, and the last of the rationing which had informed life, in '50s Britain; instead, there was more personal freedom, more disposable income and more time-saving gadgets. Cars were allowing people to be much more mobile and adventurous, televisions were making people more worldly and much more accessible and persuadable, with commercial advertisements on our screens every fifteen minutes or so.

A relatively healthy economy allowed more efficient production techniques, the price of consumer goods to fall as a consequence, and employers to pay higher wages.

1960s adverts promoting a flood of new products and holidays.

Health and hygiene were improved by the development of new consumer disinfectants and detergents, while Unilever led the way in scientific research on a wide variety of products, not least oils and fats. Canning, freezing and drying heralded the arrival of convenience foods; white goods became more efficient and kitchen-friendly because they were more compact. More women were going out to work – they needed time-saving devices to enable them to do this and raise a family at the same time. Unilever introduced the computer into the workplace, scientists were admitted onto corporate boards, supermarkets became the place to shop, packaging and advertising were crucial in influencing the decision as to which brand to buy. The first supermarkets featured food cabinets made from tough Perspex left over from the Second World War bomber factories and, of course, refrigerated units. In 1962 there were 12,000 or so supermarkets; this rose to 24,000 by 1967.

Keeping a clean house was still paramount, a reaction perhaps to the squalor and privations the previous generations were forced to endure in the urban slums clustered around pollution-belching factories. Fastidious interior housework apart, the cleaning of the step, or donkey-stoning, was an important ritual. It reflected, for the rest of the street to see, the overall cleanliness of a family – physically and morally. A donkey stone was a tablet of ground stone dust, cement and bleach badged with a donkey: first you wet your step, then you scrub it vigorously with said donkey stone. Dazzling white nets and sparkling clean windows were equally crucial. In the '50s, the perfect housewife spent an estimated fifteen hours a day cooking, cleaning and mothering. Vacuum cleaners, fridges, food mixers, toasters, irons and washing machines made the drudgery of housework that much easier and less time-consuming as the '60s progressed. The ceremony of the donkey stone gave the conscientious house-proud housewife an opportunity for gossip, to catch up on all the local news – the Facebook and Twitter of her day. Reputations were made, and shattered, on those doorsteps. The '60s saw this begin to come to an end, slowly.

The old wives' tales and urban myths were being swept away, again slowly. Girls who were 'cursed' were still prohibited from playing with boys; from bathing; from washing their hair or from sitting on cold steps, clean as the steps might be; just in case they did irreparable damage to their insides and compromised their fertility. Nearly a quarter of girls failed to benefit from any sex education at all, 40 per cent of married couples at the beginning of the decade lived with mothers- and fathers-in-law, divorce was anathema for most and punishable for some by burning in hell. Marriage was the aim, sexual intercourse was the price you paid for marrying – but it often led to those all-important babies. Little had changed since Roman times when the good Roman wife – the unobtrusive matrona – was seen and not heard, looking after the house, doing the sewing and raising the children while husband went out to work and came home to be met by his tea on the table and a wife who had done her best to prettify herself for him. No wonder that this stifling and chauvinistic way of life turned a number of women to feminism in its various forms, but this was later in the decade and in the '70s.

Illegitimacy was still stigmatic and shameful. Birth out of wedlock could give rise to life-long ostracism from society and family alike, for both mother and child. We hear of pregnant brides being showered with ashes instead of confetti, of lives blighted by and lived in simmering anger at having been abandoned on hospital doorsteps. Today, almost half of births are to unmarried mothers: the drift towards tolerance and the removal of the hypocrisy towards, and the stain of, illegitimacy began in the '60s. In 1959 the Mental Deficiency Act was finally repealed. This antediluvian legislation was passed in 1913 when one child in twenty-four was born a bastard; it allowed 'serial offenders' – women who had more than one illegitimate child – to be branded moral imbeciles and institutionalised. Men were nowhere to be seen. Indeed, one man wrote to *The Times* in 1961 blaming the apparent decline in moral standards on the gradual emancipation of women. Masquerading as sisters or aunts, the unmarried mother was still very much in evidence in the 1960s.

We often associate the '60s with a tidal wave of permissiveness, 'free' love and recreational drugs. The introduction of Gregory Pincus' hormonal oral contraceptive, Enovid, is responsible for much of this myth, supposedly heralding 'the era of the pill'. Family breakdown, family break-up and permissiveness were, to many, all due to the pill. While Victorian attitudes and hypocrisies regarding sex in particular were indeed finally shrugged off, the statistics tell a different and more restrained story. By 1961, despite confusion in the Catholic Church, 1.2 million Americans were taking Enovid allegedly for irregular menstrual cycles, the indication it assumed in order to win FDA approval. But in the UK, even at the end of the decade, only 19 per cent of married couples under forty-five used the pill while 29 per cent persisted with the condom, a massive 37 per cent still used no contraceptive at all, withdrawal was still the name of the game for many. This was despite the sterling work carried out by the Brooks Clinics, from 1964, educating women in family planning and prescribing. The pill enjoyed its real popular success in the '70s.

Rising disposable income was a significant marker of the '60s. In 1951 the average weekly wage for a man over twenty years of age was £8.30; by 1961 this had nearly doubled to £15.35, increasing to £20.30 in 1966 and to £28.05 by 1970. Some of this was offset by inflation (prices rose by 88 per cent between 1955 and 1969) but, by and large, there was a lot more money in your pocket. Even so, while the cost of food was going up, the cost of cars, televisions and white goods was coming down. Not that everyone had a fridge – only 33 per cent in 1962 and 69 per cent in 1971 – the pantry was still important. Nevertheless, the fridge and the fridge-freezer changed the way women shopped. The daily trudge to the grocers, bakers and butchers became less necessary as food was bought increasingly from supermarkets and could be stored for much longer. Televisions were becoming prevalent; their early '50s scarcity had disappeared by 1961 when 75 per cent of us watched one and this rose to 91 per cent in 1971. Colour TV programmes started on BBC Two in 1967, joined by the two other available channels, BBC One and ITV, in 1969. Washing day scrubbing and beating was a thing of the past by the end of the decade for the 64 per cent of people who possessed a washing machine. The telephone was the 'Johnny come lately', even with subscriber trunk dialling from 1961 only 4.2 million households had a phone in the house in 1966; more than half of all households were still phoneless in 1969. Queuing in the cold and wet, finding loose change and pressing button 'B' was till the norm for most people.

One of the consequences of more pounds in your pocket was that parents could indulge their children more; toy and board game manufacturers exploited this burgeoning market to the full. Barbie and Ken came over from the States and never left, although they were soon up against our very own Sindy in 1963 – 'the doll you love to dress'. Sindy displayed some of the rebellion characteristics of the decade for she was 'the free swinging, grown-up girl who dresses the way she likes'. Action Man followed Barbie over in 1966 but they were never an item; nevertheless, he did have our boys dressing and undressing dolls instead of playing cowboys and Indians. More stereotypical was Scalextric racing cars – forever breaking down and crashing. Dr Who branded toys were a great hit – to match the 'behind the sofa' TV series which came on air in 1963.

Fish fingers and pre-packed steaks became increasingly popular and were an indicator of the growing popularity of convenience foods; fish and chips wrapped in yesterday's papers remained a favourite but, by and large, food was getting faster, accounting for 20 per cent of all foods bought in 1960 rising to 25 per cent in 1970. Vesta curries were launched in 1961. Sliced bread was, literally, the best thing since sliced bread – a revolution in sandwich-making for the busy mother. What it lacked in taste (everything) the sandwich made up for in convenience; by 1969 forty-two million white-sliced loaves were being eaten every week.

A section of '60s toys, including a Sindy doll in the Castle Museum, York. (Courtesy of York Museum Trust)

Car ownership accelerated in the '60s, rising from 5,650,000 in 1960 (28 per cent of households) to 11,802,000 (about 45 per cent) in 1970, but despite all that mobility the '60s motorway (there were 600 miles of it by 1969) and trunk road building has proved sadly inadequate. Beeching took his axe to the railways, reducing the network from 13,000 miles to 11,000 and plunging us into 'almost a return to preindustrial conditions' from which many of the regions and their towns have yet to recover. Trams had all gone by 1962 (the last being in Glasgow) although trolleybuses survived until the end of the decade. Travelling from east to west and back again remains no better than when enjoyed by the Victorians, by both road and rail. Domestic air travel doubled from 1,000 million passenger kilometres between 1961 and 1971 but despite that we still lack an effective regional airport network. The '60s can be seen as a missed opportunity when it comes to travel infrastructure.

The explosion in car ownership and car journeys brought with it a certain amount of danger, and death. In 1966 a shocking 7,985 people died on the roads in the days before realistic MOTs, compulsory seat belts and breathalysers. This compares with 1,713 in 2013. Something obviously had to be done and so it was that MOTs were introduced in 1967 for cars over three years old (it had been ten years since 1961) the 70 mph speed limit was introduced, the wearing of seat belts became mandatory and the breath test came into force, and with it the stigma associated with drink-driving. By 1980 the death toll had fallen to 5,953.

The Campaign for Nuclear Disarmament peaked in 1960 with between 25 and 30 per cent of the population supporting its cause; admittedly it was largely middle and upper class in make-up but, significantly, it included many housewives among its members. What we today call media celebrities became ever younger, with stars such as David Hockney and David Bailey leading the way: *That Was the Week That Was* and *Private Eye* were at the fore of the 'satire boom'. The working classes were proving themselves adept champions of a new Britain, with regional accents and characters fashionable in art, actors, soaps and films. For example Tom Courtenay, *Kes*, *Saturday Night and Sunday Morning*, *Coronation Street*, *Z Cars*, *Room at the Top*, Ian Sillitoe, Hockney and Eddie Waring. The seminal work of the decade was Richard Hoggart's *Uses of Literacy*; Hoggart was a graduate of Leeds University, working at the University of Hull when he published his classic in 1957. Hoggart described with lucidity the working class as it really was, rather than just 'a figment of upper class intellectual imagination'.

The '50s had seen the explosive and exciting explosion of popular music through the early recordings of Bill Haley, Elvis Presley and others. This continued apace into the '60s with the ubiquitous juke box, 45 rpm single and the 33⅓ rpm LP replacing sheet music as the measure of all things musically successful, and championing the development of electronics and recording techniques. Indeed, popular music was to produce an enduring and indelible soundtrack to the decade, showcasing extraordinary musicianship and mature song-writing skills in countless very young new and constantly emerging stars. We may never see such an explosion of youthful talent again as Goffin and King, Bob Dylan, Simon and Garfunkel, Tamla Motown, Ray Davies, Neil Young and Joni Mitchell. Once again, the north proved just as capable as the south: Beatles, Moody Blues, and Hollies up against Rolling Stones, Dave Clark 5 and The Who. And it was not just popular music per se: rhythm and blues (John Mayall and his revolving Bluesbreakers), folk (Sandy Denny and Fairport Convention), rock (Deep Purple, Led Zeppelin and Free), so-called psychedelia (Pink Floyd and Procul Harum) and country (Glen Campbell and Jimmy Webb) were all in the final mix. It was fuelled by the emergence of offshore pirate radio in 1961; Radio Caroline took to the airwaves in 1964, joining Radio Luxembourg which had been broadcasting since 1933 but was coming into its own in 1964. There was also, from June 1966 until 14 August 1967, the popular Dutch Radio 270 moored off Scarborough on board the refurbished trawler, *The Oceaan-7*. Apparently, there were four million listeners at peak times.

The '60s saw the demise of the popular circulating libraries and the two-penny libraries. Where was the reader to obtain books now? Public libraries were established and proved a big hit, from 1964 'the national health service for books', bookshops were opened to satisfy the increasing demand for Allan Lane's affordable paperbacks: the Penguin and the Pelican. Penguins were joined on the ever-bulging shelves by other imprints such as Pan, Fontana and, for children, Puffins. Although we were the biggest library lenders in the world with 30 per cent of the population owning a library ticket, we lagged far behind the US and the rest of Europe in terms of books read. In 1963 we published 2,375 new novels – a mere 200 up from the 2,153 published in 1937. 90 per cent of all books were sold to libraries.

Paul Rodgers (later of Free and Queen) here on the right with the other Road Runners in 1965 on the back of an iconic 1954 Ford Consul convertible. Photo courtesy of Colin Bradley, formerly of the Road Runners. It was taken outside Joe Bradley's home in Brentford Road in Norton. The Road Runners are, left to right, Dave Usher, Colin Bradley, Micky Moody and Paul Rodgers. The little girl in the gateway is Joe's niece Sharon Jacques (now Sharon Stewart).

It is something of an urban myth that the ingestion or, less frequently, the injection of recreational drugs was a hallmark of the '60s. Drugs were indeed taken, in copious quantities, but they were by no means the exclusive preserve of the so-called 'people of the 1960s' – the young, purveyors of art and music, and students – although you were as likely to see and smell cannabis at a concert in a university campus as anywhere. Amphetamines had been taken by adults in the '50s as indeed they were by aircrew and soldiers during the Second World War, needle drugs were the narcotics of choice for adults in the '50s while cannabis was a useful analgesic from at least Victorian days. Mods and musicians did much for the market for recreational drugs, but they were not the revolution in just the young man's or young woman's head they are sometimes purported to be. Cannabis did indeed become very popular, as did lysergic acid and other mind-expanders, but, like sex and 'free love', they were probably talked about by the country's youth as much as indulged in. Cannabis in particular was enjoyed, but not just by young people outside pubs and inside college halls of residence. Research shows that a spliff was shared among many an older middle-class professional, including college teachers. In 1968 the Wooton Committee found that there may have been as many as 300,000 cannabis sativa users in the UK; in 1971 research estimates up to two million. Generally speaking the authorities met all of this with panic and hysteria, even the establishment *Times* felt obliged to restore a sense of reasonable moderation when it published its Rees-Mogg leader, *Who breaks a butterfly upon a wheel?*, arguing against the overreaction when Mick Jagger and Keith Richards were jailed for possession in 1967.

Increasing levels of crimes of violence were a hallmark of the '60s, particularly among the eight (!) to twenty-one age groups. Increases of 11 per cent per year were the norm with 11,592 cases reported in 1960 and 21,046 in 1968. How far this was a reflection of increased reporting or of intrinsic criminality it is hard to tell, but it is clear that violent crime was on the up. Dixon of Dock Green was by now more *Z Cars* (and then the *Sweeney* in the '70s). Rare and sensationally repellent events such as the Great Train Robbery in 1963, the Moors Murders in 1965, the Shepherd's Bush police killings in 1966 and the Kray twins' trial in 1969 only went to show the depths to which the seriously criminal could stoop. In October 1965 Roy Jenkins introduced an Act of Parliament banning capital punishment on a five-year trial. After three years it was obvious which way the country should go and the ban was made permanent in 1969.

The association of the '60s with a much more liberal moral code, indeed with permissiveness, is reflected in a number of significant legal landmark decisions and Acts of Parliament. The first, in 1961, was the *Lady Chatterley's Lover* trial in which it was deemed fine for us to enjoy this book with its sexual content intact, but not before the oafish defence exemplified much that was (still) wrong in our society when he asked the jury if they would be comfortable knowing their servants might read the book. In 1967 the Liberal MP David Steel successfully steered the Abortion Act through the House, thus offering the average woman a choice where before there was none – she could now have an abortion so long as it was agreed by two medical doctors on medical and psychological grounds. NHS clinics opened to meet the demand and drove away much of the dangerous, illegal back-street abortions or the obligation to keep an unwanted baby. The film *Alfie* exemplifies the situation well. That same year the NHS were obliged to provide contraceptives and family planning advice.

The Sexual Offences Act of 1967 ended much of the monstrous prejudice suffered by homosexuals when it decriminalised homosexual acts between two consenting adults in private, and with it the blackmail sometimes endured by homosexuals. The 1963 Pinter film *The Servant* illustrates the pre-1967 clandestine situation.

Ken Loach's 1966 *Cathy Come Home* was described as 'an ice-pick in the brain' when it was watched by twelve million viewers, 25 per cent of the adult population. The TV play tackled issues taboo to the British public: homelessness, the right of women to keep their children, unemployment, and the role of the social services. Some of these issues remain unresolved today but the play did succeed in radically changing attitudes to homelessness and gave Shelter a much needed springboard.

The long-overdue overhauling of the divorce laws in 1969 – dragging them into the twentieth century – had the added benefits of finally recognising women as independent individuals and of valuing their contribution to the family home (either as housewife or money earner) on a par with the husband's. 'Irretrievable breakdown' released thousands of women and men from loveless, sometimes abusive, marriages. From now on the family wealth would be shared. The Divorce Reform Act never amounted to 'a Casanova's Charter' as some feminists feared. As to be expected, divorces were at 51,000 per year in 1969 – ten times the number in 1959. Indeed, despite the prevalence of another myth, feminism was never a great force in '60s Britain. Indeed, what some might view as anti-feminist – the mini skirt and hot pants – were much more in evidence. The single-most important example of feminism of the time was probably the publication of Germaine Greer's *The Female Eunuch* in 1970. *Spare Rib* was not launched until 1972 – its aims and scope was to explore and 'present alternatives to the traditional gender roles for women as virgin, wife or mother', but not in the '60s.

In the '60s, higher education was overhauled quite dramatically, with colleges of technology becoming polytechnics and new universities established at York, Sussex, Essex, Lancaster, Kent, Stirling and Warwick. The virtual abolition of grammar schools began in 1965 with the responsibility for comprehensive provision loaded onto local authorities, leading to wholesale inconsistency and confusion. Perhaps the greatest leap forward, though, was the opening of the Open University in 1969, a ground-breaking distance learning and research university making higher education open to all.

Despite the innate xenophobia displayed by the British, foreign food, foreign restaurants and the drinking of wine were becoming more acceptable, but still only to a small sector of (middle class) society. Foreign holidays were responsible for increased wine drinking and eating foreign food; in 1960 we were each drinking less than two litres of wine a year – next to nothing – but by 1969 this had increased to four litres. Before package holidays olive oil was something you bought from the chemist, but in the '60s it migrated to the supermarket or the grocer's. In 1960 there were only six 'Indian' restaurants in the UK (mostly run by Bangladeshis); in 1970 there were 1,200.

The class system, despite all the changes, was still alive and well with a '60s survey showing that 67 per cent of respondents classed themselves as working class, 29 per cent middle class; one 25-stone eccentric respondent was 'sporting class'. If the survey reveals anything, it demonstrates a real awareness of the social division dictated by type of work. In the late '60s Labour's Richard Crossman still felt comfortable describing his life as marked by a 'facility of freedom and an amplitude of life which cuts us off from the vast mass of people'.

In the '60s trade union membership grew for both men and women; for men it was 56 per cent of all male employees in 1961 rising to 58 per cent in 1971, for women in the same years it was 24 per cent and 32 per cent. As with today, immigration was unpopular among the indigenous population (and presumably earlier immigrants). In the 1960s some 80 per cent of people surveyed believed there were too many immigrants in the country, unmindful of the massive contribution (as today) they make at all levels of the British economy, from vegetable pickers to cardiovascular surgeons. 1968 saw the alarming rise of the National Front and an alarmist Enoch Powell envisaged Virgil's 'rivers of blood'.

The institution of the family, the glue which binds us all together, remained largely unchanged in the 1960s. The sad ravages of the Second World War had still not worked themselves through and there were still many more widows than widowers. Marriage at an earlier age was increasingly popular. Divorces, not surprisingly now that women were legally-speaking on a level playing field, were up from 45,794 in 1968 to 58,239 in 1970. The birth rate rose to 18.8 per thousand of the total population from 16 per cent in the early 1950s. As with the '50s, men never had it so good, literally. In general there were many more women than men (28,562,000 women compared with 26,952,000 men) but in the crucial sexually active years between fifteen and twenty-nine, things were beginning to change. In 1951 women outnumbered men 5,255,000 to 5,073,000, in 1961 there were 5,159,000 men and boys compared to 5,100,000 women and girls and by the end of the decade the halcyon days for men were well and truly over with 5,915,000 men and only 5,764,000 women.

The '60s might be described as the decade when fathers began to take on a more accepting, less formal and paternal role in the family – sharing the upbringing of the children more because they were increasingly often not the sole breadwinners. Children were more likely to be treated with respect, with their views taken into consideration to some extent.

The 1969 survey, Sex and Marriage in England Today makes fascinating reading. 24 per cent of married couples met at a dance, 15 per cent at work, 12 per cent at parties and 12 per cent through mutual friends. 86 per cent of women were in love, but only a disappointing 74 per cent of men, similarly 26 per cent of men were expressively not in love, and 11 per cent of women. This, of course, takes no notice of the 'I'm Not in Love' factor, saying you're not when you are. 26 per cent of men and 63 per cent of women were virgins early on their wedding nights; more equably, 20 per cent of men and 26 per cent of women married the person with whom they first had sexual intercourse. Anecdotally, some girls and women still believed that pregnancy was impossible if you 'did it' standing up, and that you had to actually fall asleep with your partner before you could be said to have 'slept' with him or her. More reassuringly, 67 per cent of women now said that sex was very important in marriage as against 65 per cent of men.

We have seen how the use of contraceptives was rejected by many young couples. This naturally led to a significant rise in the number of illegitimate births, from 5–8 per cent of all births in 1961 to 8.2 per cent by the early '70s, an indication not just of heightened permissiveness but also perhaps of the increasing acceptance of illegitimacy in some areas of British society. Still, we have noted how many of the 40,000 girls and women who found themselves with babies born outside marriage every year were cruelly ostracised by their families and by society; in general they were treated appallingly, not least by the church. Many of the infants had to be surrendered for adoption. Sexless marriages were not that uncommon due often to a general lack of sex education, sometimes this fostered what we now call erectile dysfunction and revulsion towards or fear of sex, in both women and men.

In the 1960s the first NHS hearing aids were dispensed, the new £1 note was issued, Penguin published *Lady Chatterley's Lover* in a 200,000 print run after their victory in the obscenity trial in 1965, the first 'moving pavement' started rolling at Bank station. In 1961 Conovid, the first contraceptive pill for the UK market went on sale; Yuri Gagarin was rocketed into space, following a dog; betting shops were legalised, MOTs were introduced, the millionth Morris Minor came off the production line and immigration controls were introduced. Viv Nicholson won the equivalent today of £3.5 million on the Pools and kept her promise to 'spend, spend, spend' until it was all gone. In 1962 the Cuban missile crisis scared the life out of everybody, American John Glen orbited the earth and the Telstar satellite sent live TV signals across the Atlantic. In 1963 Kennedy was assassinated, the Great Train robbery was committed and the BBC stopped banning sex, politics, religion and royalty from comedy shows. In 1964 Harold Wilson became PM after thirteen years of Conservative rule, mods and rockers fought it out on Clacton beach, BBC Two opened up with *Play School* and the mini-skirt arrived. In 1965 cigarette smoking stopped being good for you and tobacco advertising was banned from TV, Britain's tallest building – the Post Office Tower – opened at 620 feet, Churchill died, the Rent Act imposed rent control, the death penalty was abolished, the first Race Relations Act came into force, Moors murderers were tried and Mary Whitehouse established the National Viewers' and Listeners' Association. In 1966 the tragic Aberfan landslide killed 144, mainly school children; England won the World Cup and Barclaycard was introduced – the first credit card. The year 1967 saw the first North Sea oil pumped ashore at Easington in Durham, abortion was legalised, BBC Radio One went on air with 'Flowers in the Rain' and Tony Blackburn, and private homosexual acts between consenting couples over twenty-one were legalised. In 1968 Martin Luther King was assassinated in Memphis and the age of adulthood was reduced from twenty-one to eighteen. In 1969 Neil Armstrong was seen walking on the moon, the voting age was reduced from twenty-one to eighteen, Concorde made its maiden flight, 'irretrievable breakdown' was allowed as grounds for divorce and female workers at Ford Dagenham won equal pay with men. New words entered the English language: 'miniskirt' in 1965, and 'Cultural

Revolution', inspired by Mao's *Little Red Book*. New charities first saw the light of day in the '60s or continued to thrive: Oxfam (founded in 1942), War on Want (1951), Amnesty International (1961) and Shelter (1966).

Britain, of course, was influenced and impacted by many external events and forces in the 1960s. The British Army, air force and navy were engaged, not always honourably, in operations in Malaya, Kenya, Aden, Borneo, Oman and, from 1969, Northern Ireland. The Cold War was 'fought' by the British Army on the Rhine and MI6. National Service had ended in 1960, while the troubles in Cyprus had come to an end in 1959. 400 National Servicemen were killed in action with many more wounded between 1948 and 1960.

The word iconic is about as overused now as that lame adjective 'nice' was in the '60s. Iconoclastically, 'iconic' is now often used to describe the ordinary, bland and humdrum – people as well as places and events. However, some of the events of the 1960s which informed how we continued to live and saw the world can truly be described as 'iconic'. The television and cinema newsreels brought the world much, much closer: we could see what was going on beyond our shores in our very living rooms. The building of the Berlin Wall and the Iron Curtain, the assassination of John Kennedy, the death of Marilyn Monroe, dogs in space, men in space, England winning the World Cup in 1966, the assassination of Martin Luther King, civil rights in the USA, student riots in Paris and the Vietnam War – all these global iconic moments, and not a few more, were that much more tangible and somehow more experiential.

When smoking was still good for you ...   The Brandenburg Gate on the Berlin Wall.

Chapter 2

1960s York and The Esher Vision

After the war, it was government policy to seduce local authorities with generous subsidies to induce them to build high into the sky, in order to replace bombed-out or derelict properties and so ease the housing shortage. York's low-level skyscape, quite unique in a city of its size, is due in part to one Labour Alderman Bill Burke, Chairman of the Housing Committee. Burke famously retorted to an offer of 'subsidies' made at a council meeting, 'Over my dead body will we have bloody tower blocks in York.' Burke can be ranked with The Civic Trust, Etty, Evelyn and Sir Walter Scott as a valiant and jealous preserver of the city's heritage and character, in the face of couldn't-care-less

The '60s sitting room in the Sixties Gallery in the Castle Museum. (Courtesy of York Museums Trust)

The sitting room constructed by Hunter &
Smallpage in their shop.

perpetrators of civic vandalism who seem intent on blighting every age. Just look at the
Stonebow and that obtrusive hotel on the banks of the Ouse. As a footnote it is worth
pointing out that Burke was not all heart, when Lord Esher in 1967 came to the city
(surreptitiously to avoid the press and a hostile council) Burke told him bluntly, 'We
don't like consultants here.'

In January 1966 Richard Crossman – the Minister for Housing and Local
Government – expressed anxieties over the destruction of many of Britain's historic
towns due to 'rampant commercial development'. He felt there was a failure to reflect
the design, materials and scale of surroundings, which was destroying the beauty and
character of many historic towns. His actual words at the time were 'exactly the same
damn thing is being plonked down in town after town, the same sort of supermarket
beside the cathedral.' He announced pilot projects where four historic towns would
be examined to discover how best to reconcile preservation and progress. *The Times*
endorsed the need for the plan: 'If confirmation is required, rebuilding in the centre
of York provided it in a sharp and painful form.' In 1968 a report was published by
the Minister for Housing and Local Government and the local council entitled *York:
A Study in Conservation*, and was one of four reports (the others were of Chichester,
Chester and Bath; King's Lynn failed to make it) seeking answers to the often vexed
question as to how to bring these cities into the later twentieth century without actually
knocking most of them down. One of Crossman's criteria in the final choice was that
he was keen to help towns and cities which had already demonstrated that they had
helped themselves. Now, as we know, it was a bit late for some of York's streets and
buildings, but this report, under the aegis of Lord Esher, perversely restricted to the
area within the city walls, and its new enlightened attitude shines important light on
'60s York and provides a snapshot of the city during that decade. As with Seebohm
Rowntree's fascinating *English Life and Leisure* which focuses on York in the '50s,
it gives us a fund of almost unique research into '60s York. Esher's fee was a princely
£20,000 – half paid by the government, half by the city.

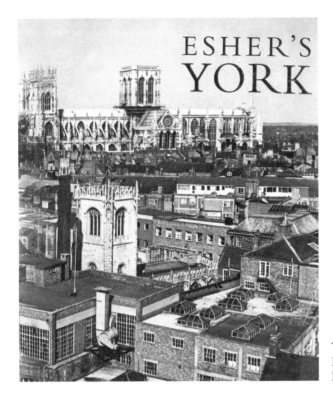

The supplement of the Esher Report published by the York Press.

Esher had five objectives: that the commercial heart of York should remain alive and be able to compete on equal terms with other cities; that the elimination of decay, traffic congestion and noise should so improve the environment that the centre will again become a very attractive place to live, for families, students and retired people; that land uses conflicting with these purposes must gradually be removed from the walled city; that York's historic character should be so enhanced and the best of its buildings maintained so that they become 'economically self-serving', and that 'erection of new buildings of any but the highest architectural standards should cease' within the walls.

However, Esher had concerns over the council's reaction, as did *The Architects Journal*, one of the gold standards of its day: 'If York fails to respond, the whole exercise must be written off and all hopes of making a serious start on conserving what is most beautiful and valuable in this country can be abandoned as a romantic dream.'

Esher had a 'difficult' relationship with York Corporation who imposed stringent conditions even before his study was allowed. Bizarrely, it should be limited to the area inside the city walls. They favoured an inner ring road while most experts and the public were pressing for an outer ring, and the council were not experts. One lame, frankly disingenuous, excuse they later advanced for reluctance in accepting his report, even in principle, was that he had not considered the area outside the walls! The other three towns had accepted their reports much sooner. York Corporation remained stubbornly intransigent and ignorance, xenophobia and exclusiveness nearly won the day. A review of the report in the RIBA Journal, the other gold standard and authoritative journal of the Royal Institute of British Architects (26 February 1969) tells us that Lord Esher regretted the decision, backed by the city council, to confine the conservation study to the part of the city within the walls, 'partly because there are some splendid historic streets beyond this area which deserve study, but equally because an official plan to run a ring road directly outside the walls seems lamentably mistaken both from the point of view of successfully conserving the walled city, and that of its separation from the rest of the town'.

Esher responded to the opposition his report was facing:

Strict development control from now on could prevent any further horrors from going up in the city while the long-tem job is being done ... While we were working on the study the city sent us all planning applications for consideration. But that procedure came to an end the day the report was finished, and now development control is back on the old system, which failed to prevent some pretty bad buildings going up in the past. One or two decisions have already been taken which wholly conflict with my proposals.

He wisely proposed the appointment of a director with responsibility for conservation. 'Otherwise I see very disappointing results coming from the government's efforts to encourage conservation.'

Reconstruction and preservation: Rougier Street in 1960 (*overleaf*), 1963 and 1968, Newbiggin Street, Groves Lane 1964 and Newgate 1966. (Photos courtesy of York Press)

York Civic Trust did much to save the day, their website sums up the controversy:

There was some reluctance by the City Council to participate in the project, but the York Civic Trust offered to share the Council's proportion of the fee. That gesture resulted in the Council supporting the project. The Study was published in February 1969 and created a vision which was to influence many future policies. Not all Esher's proposals were accepted, but we have him to thank for encouraging more residential properties within the City Centre including new houses in the Aldwark area, and the rehabilitation of the Bishophill area. He also advocated the extension of the pedestrianisation of much of the central area of the City.

Esher, as we have seen, recognised the threat cars and lorries posed to the city's historic fabric and called for Bootham Bar to be closed to traffic, access to be restricted through Micklegate Bar and only residents' cars allowed through Walmgate and Monk Bars. Four multi-storey car parks should be built outside the walls providing 5000 off-street parking spaces (there were only 190 within the walls at the time of the report).

Monk Bar being decorated in 1961 for the royal wedding.

George Street Bar restoration in 1961.

Left: Stuck in Micklegate Bar in 1969: this 20-foot-long lorry was stuck there for three hours with its load of fertiliser. One witness was reported as saying 'I wouldn't mind if he was a foreigner but he's only come from Malton.'

Below: The Bar Walls at station Avenue with some rather fine '60s cars.

The plan proposed an extension of pedestrianisation throughout the walled city. 'York is exceptionally rich in narrow streets ideal for pedestrianisation' the report points out: 'In secret alleys known only to the native or the inquisitive explorer, and in the elevated circuit of the walls and bars, which though incomplete could easily be made more accessible and more enjoyable'. The major areas targeted for pedestrianisation were around the minster precinct, throughout the central shopping area, in a wide arc through King's Manor and round Micklegate.

Once traffic was sorted, the problems of conservation itself could be addressed. 'All that has been done to rescue historic York in the past twenty years has been first-aid', the report says frankly. But inevitably 'there will be a gap between what the market will bear and what the environment should be, and this gap can be closed only by public spending on a scale now normal in other European countries but still grossly inadequate here.'

Esher divided the city within the walls into eight sectors, each with clearly differentiated individual qualities, its own life and ambience:

Micklegate-Bishophill, the old Roman Colonia south-west of the river, with the historic entry to the city, Micklegate Bar.

The central shopping sector, of which the report comments that 'it contains one of the prettiest luxury shopping streets in the world (Stonegate)' and 'has so far baffled the big developers'.

A foggy day in '60s York. (Photo courtesy of York Press)

Stonegate in 1963. (Photo courtesy of York Press)

The Minster precinct, with the Minster rising out of narrow medieval streets and cobbled lanes. One proposal was to open up the underground reservoir here and make a water feature in the park.

The King's Manor area, 'tacked onto the western edge of the historic city' and containing its art gallery, library, theatre, museum, 'a romantic riverside park' and the sixteenth-century King's Manor buildings. Exhibition Square has huge potential as a central feature of the city but, sadly, the council failed to react to the proposal and, to this day, remains a missed opportunity with too much concrete, not enough green, and too many old diesel-belching tourist buses.

Aldwark, to the east, is a total contrast: 'silent, deserted, its last Georgian houses falling into decay, its half-empty workshops and warehouses awaiting clearance' close to the Minster.

Foss Islands, the industrial sector, 'York's back yard. Dominated by a fine cooling tower and by the great warehouse still in use, rising sheer out of the … Foss, this sector makes a by no means unworthy contribution to the variety of the York scene.'

Walmgate, defined by the Foss and the curve of the city walls 'its backbone village street with twin churches and its industrial hinterland'. Low-lying, with a long history of congestion and squalor, slum clearance and municipal housing are in progress here and garages and new offices form 'the least attractive of all entries into the walled city'.

Right: Tower House in Ogleforth. (Photo courtesy of York Press)

Below: The De Grey Rooms. (Photo courtesy of York Press)

Gillygate and Lord Mayor's Walk in 1961. (Photo courtesy of York Press)

Walmgate properties in 1966. (Photo courtesy of York Press)

The Castle sector, 'traffic-ridden and car infested but full of character and potentiality, with the finest Gothic spire and several of the most handsome Georgian buildings in the city, as well as a gloomily romantic Victorian street'.

One unexpected revelation, particularly germane to Petergate, was the large number of redundant upper storeys above shops which were either used only for storage or not at all. In fact 144 in all, in some cases even the stairs, had been boarded up or removed. These offered significant potential for university student lodgings, to help bolster the inner walls population and the great enrichment of the life of the city in general.

Astonishingly, the report also found that despite the fact that 'the City Council has spent more on conservation and restoration of its heritage than any city of comparable resources in the United Kingdom', thirty-two listed buildings had been demolished since 1954, despite the efforts of Georgian Society and others in the city to retain them. Even more astonishing when York, in fact, was one of only eight towns in England and Wales that provided an annual sum in grants to occupiers to help maintain historic buildings. One can only speculate as to what on earth was going on.

RIBA continued:

> But despite these efforts the disease of urban blight can be seen in all its stages in the walled city. In Aldwark and St Andrew-gate it has reached the advanced stage where only comprehensive redevelopment connect the case; in Walmgate industrial encroachment at the back and traffic in front have for many years been inexorably exerting the same pressures and in Micklegate one can see precisely the same disease at an earlier stage.

Many of the splendid town houses in the area were now constrained by industry.

Petergate.

Knocking down part of Botterills in 1962. Built in 1884 next to Lendal Bridge, it was reduced in height by half in 1965 when it became a car dealership. Patrick Nuttgens described the original building as 'an exotic red and yellow Byzantine building with ramps inside, up which the horses were led to their stalls – a kind of multi-story horse car park'. It was frequently used by patrons of the 1868 Yorkshire Club for gentlemen (River House) in from the country, just over Lendal Bridge.

Even by 1968 it was recognised that the two major twentieth-century developments – Piccadilly (1912) and Stonebow (1960) – were major culprits in the malaise that had affected York and, indeed, gave rise to the very need for such a report, if only to stop the disease spreading. By the 1960s York was widely recognised as 'one of the richest and most complex townscapes in the world. It is the most medieval in feeling of all English cities, a city of streets rather than spaces', so patently something had to be done. Urban depopulation was a global phenomenon and York was no different. In 1965 the population within the walls was a mere 3,576 – a full one third of its medieval population – and as low as 3,498 in 1961, the all-time low. Even the new university could not help, with only thirty-one students out of 900 living within the walls. It is estimated that 175,000 people came into the city to shop in a '60s year, the main economic activity of the centre.

Visitors were indeed important in the '60s but could have been much more so. York spent more per head of population on its museums than any other city in the UK. In return, the Castle Museum had 657,000 visitors in 1966 compared with 980,000 at the British Museum in London. In York 85 per cent came in the six summer months; overall half were visitors from Yorkshire, one in forty from overseas. The illuminating Castle Museum's Sixties Gallery portrays what life would have been like in York; the website tells us:

The gallery uses fascinating and iconic objects from our social history, art, fashion, military and astronomy collections to bring back the atmosphere of change which swept over the country during the 1960s. Highlights include a Lambretta scooter, a Dansette record player, Beatles singles and fashion by Mary Quant. Using visual design and colour schemes influenced by the trends of the decade, it explores key themes such as fashion, music, the home, sport, childhood, the Space Race, free love, counterculture and women's liberation.

Two views of the 'swinging sixties gallery' in the Castle Museum showing such icons as Twiggy, a scooter and a US space capsule. (Courtesy of York Museums Trust)

The Yorkshire Museum and the National Railway Museum both did very well compared with similar museums elsewhere. The bad news was that most (90 per cent) of the visitors only came for the day with the concomitant short period of time in which to spend money in the city. Not surprising, though, considering that hotel accommodation was lamentable, with only ninety-two hotel rooms out 540 sampled having en-suite facilities. In 1950 there were rooms in hotels and guest houses for 1,300 visitors, rising to 1,900 in 1970. Employment in York's hotels was on a par with non-tourist Doncaster's, and only 33 per cent of that of Harrogate. More alarmingly, the number of hotel rooms in 1960s York was half that available in Bath and Chester and 25 per cent of that in nearby Harrogate. In 1967 only one in five visitors came from foreign parts, one in four stayed more than one night and two out of three came by car (reflecting the local profile of visitors); 888,000 visitors went to the Minster. Clearly, the York of the '60s was nowhere near realising its tourism potential.

An August 1967 survey of visitors revealed that out of a sample of 1,257 visitors 1,087 came from the UK and 170 from abroad. The ratio of adults to children was 11:2 for UK and foreign alike bringing the inevitable conclusion that York was not the best place to bring children. Complaints were not solicited but the surveyors got them anyway. Fourteen respondents expressed a general approval of the city and twenty-seven complained about the lack of signposting for directions within the city, car parks, public conveniences and attractions. Ten wanted more street maps and

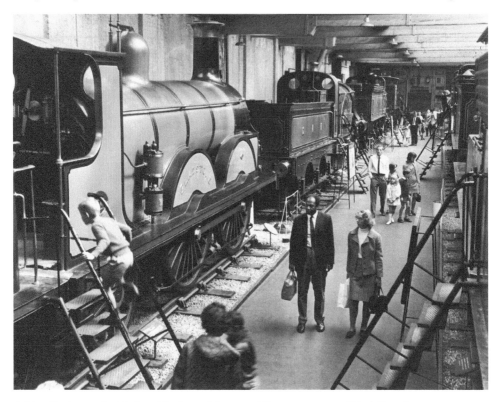

A '60s display at the National Railway Museum. (Photo courtesy of York Press)

information to be made available, eighteen bemoaned the number of shops, garages and restaurants that were closed, not least the Tourist Information Centre which closed at 5.30 p.m., just when most visitors were arriving by train or car! Some visitors used the police station as a last resort. Thirteen complained about the traffic, indicating it should be banned, especially near the Minster; seven about the lack of restaurants and nine the amount of litter. The council was reluctant to listen to Viscount Esher's detailed and robust recommendations; if they had had the humility to listen to their visitors they would have got a very similar message.

Traffic has been the bane of York since the surge in car use 39 per cent (about 1600 in 1966) of 1960s cars stopping in the city were driven by commuters with less than 5 per cent carrying shoppers – a reflection perhaps of the baneful provision of car parking in those days – a pitiful 190 off-street parking spaces. Back yards and derelict land must have been much in demand by office and shop workers.

York, of course, was (still) rich in listed buildings in the '60s. Within the walls alone, there were 106 Grade I and 438 Grade II with twenty-nine added since 1954 thanks largely to sterling work done by York Georgian Society and others. Against that, though, we need to offset a staggering thirty-two losses – nothing, it seems, could stop civic vandals wrecking the city. And this at the same time as the council spending £200,000 since the Second World War on such wonderful projects as restoring the city walls and the medieval bars, restoring the Assembly Rooms and the Red House, and reconstructing the Shambles – more money than any other comparable city in the UK.

Reconstructing a property in Shambles in 1962.

Pump Court – at the junction of King's Court and Newgate.

Pump Court was the site of one of the many water pumps and wells that served the city. John Wesley preached in a room (the 'Oven') here in 1753 (one of twenty-six visits to the city); it became an official place of worship for Methodists in 1754. One of the country's only two surviving lantern tower windows in Britain is in Pump Court, tragically, and negligently, almost hidden from public view by dustbins. Betty Petre lived here, she kept her cattle in the court before slaughter in Shambles; Mr Huber collected sheeps' guts and washed them in a drain before exporting them to Germany to make fiddle strings. Other residents included a chimney sweep and a prostitute, referred to locally as 'an old knock'.

The soon to be ubiquitous supermarket had begun its relentless march through York by the end of the '60s. The *Journal of Architecture*'s review of the Esher Report captures the professional, and popular, view very well:

Supermarkets have already moved in with their usual brashness and large scale buildings and have penetrated nearer to the heart of the city than should ever have been permitted. And in the report's large scale map showing areas of proposed change it looks as if some more scale multiples are to be allowed nearer to the core than seems to us desirable: for example such developments are apparently to be permitted all the way from near the Castle, up Piccadilly and Parliament Street to Davygate and Samson Square – the edge of that area of ancient streets and alleyways is proposed largely to pedestrianise. This worries us, not only because of the scale of the buildings but also because the demand for access to them must surely build up pressures against Lord Esher's admirable plans for limiting access for the car into the walled city. Would

Parliament Street.

it not have been wiser to confine these large new shops to the neighbourhood of the
four multi-storey car parks near the walls that are proposed in the report?
The Council's willingness to sacrifice the best of York for commercial gain was plain
for all to see – a shortcoming and unprofessionalism that is still not entirely absent
from planning decisions today.

Despite it all, the '60s saw the start of a valuable period of reconstruction and
conservation. In 1968 a number of localities would have been unrecognisable later in the
decade and through to today in 2015. Aldwark was described as 'a derelict hinterland
containing many historical buildings and in need of comprehensive redevelopment ...
silent, deserted, its last Georgian houses falling into decay, its half-empty workshops
and warehouses awaiting clearance.'

St Andrewgate was 'the most decrepit thoroughfare in central York'. Swinegate was
'a congested central commercial area in need of piecemeal redevelopment ... a mosaic
of complex activity and jumbled buildings ever since York has existed as a city ...
comprising some of York's best architecture and some of its worst.'

Micklegate, 'an historic street suffering from blight'; and Petergate, 'a typical group
of beautiful York houses in need of conversion to ensure their preservation'. It was
in the '60s that the need for renovation and preservation was first recognised and
brought to everyone's notice by Viscount Esher and, to varying degrees, acted upon
despite opposition from the council.

Swinegate. (Photo courtesy of York Press)

The Guildhall was built in 1445 on the site of the earlier 'Common Hall' dating from at least 1256. It was originally intended for the Guild of St Christopher and St George and the corporation who took over completely in 1549. Council meetings are still held there in the Victorian Council Chamber of 1891. It was used as a theatre – Richard III watched *Credo* here in 1483 – and as a Court of Justice, and was where Margaret Clitherow was tried in 1586. In 1647 during the Civil War, Cromwell agreed to pay a ransom of £200,000 to the Scots in exchange for Charles I; the money was counted here. It contains a bell captured at the Siege of Rangoon in 1851.

On 21 June 1960 York Guildhall was reopened by the Queen Mother following severe damage inflicted during the Baedeker raid on 29 April 1942. In the reconstruction a single tree trunk was used for each oak pillar, the originals coming locally from the royal Forest of Galtres. The Inner Room survived the raid intact and has panelled walls, masons' marks, two hidden stairways and a ceiling decorated with old bosses. One of the principal 1960 features was a magnificent new window, designed and painted by H. W. Harvey of York.

The window depicts the following, in order to give a fairly comprehensive picture of York history:

First we have architectural gems which feature the Minster, Merchant Adventurer's Hall, and the four bars: Monkgate, Walmgate, Bootham and Micklegate. There is a wide military history with features from Roman and Viking occupations, the Civil War siege of 1644, and the Baedeker raid in 1942. Civic matters follow with depictions of the City of York Arms, a procession and, finally, a performance of one of the Mystery Plays – *The Flood*. Commercial matters come next, the most germane to the Guildhall, illustrating a fair from the Middle Ages, a cargo ship, the railway in York, and the former Ouse Bridge, now replaced, itself a hive of commercial activity.

Religious York concludes the lights with the baptism of King Edwin, Alcuin, architect of the Carolingian renaissance and, strangely, the Assembly Rooms (which have no obvious religious connection).

The top of the window clearly depicts characters from the early ecclesiastical history of the city; they are:

> John Thornton, of Coventry (who was the man who glazed the East window of the Medieval Minster), Constantine the Great, convert to Christianity and responsible for ending the state persecution of Christians, Athelstan and William Etty. Etty was a famous and controversial York painter but he also did much good work to save the walls and various building from mindless civic vandalism. According to tradition, Athelstan, returning from the battle of Brunanburgh fought against the Vikings, observed the many poor folk maintained by the Colidei of St Peter's, York, and granted, in 936, a thrave, or twenty sheaves of corn, from every plough ploughing in the then extensive diocese of York, for the upkeep of these poor people. This is one of the earliest, if not the earliest, references to almshouses in English history.

Archbishop Walter de Gray, Lord Fairfax, Queen Philippa, King Edward III, Robinson Crusoe (who, in the first lines of Daniel Defoe's, *Robinson Crusoe*, reveals that he hailed from York) and, finally, Lord Burlington. Lord Fairfax, like Etty, saved York from further destruction during the Civil War while Lord Burlington was the designer of the Blake Street Assembly Rooms, one of Europe's first neo-classical buildings and one of the eighteenth century's most celebrated buildings. Philippa and Edward married in the Minster.

A detail from the magnificently restored window.

In 1967 a thorough survey of the Minster revealed that the building, in particular the central tower, was on the verge of collapse. £2 million was raised and spent by 1972 to reinforce the building foundations and roof. The water table had fallen due to extraction by local houses and businesses, causing the foundations to erode; the main piers of the central tower had dipped below the level of the rest of the building; the transepts were listing, the stonework was in a mess generally and the great east window was hanging perilously forward. The tower was propped up while the crypt was excavated and the building made stable.

During the excavations, remains of the north corner of the Roman Principia (headquarters of the Roman fort, Eboracum) were found under the south transept.

York Minster's organ is rightly famous. In 1960 J. W. Walker & Sons restored the actions, lowered wind pressures and introduced mutations and higher chorus work to chime with the neo-classical movement. The fire of 1829 had destroyed the previous organ; the basis of the present organ dates from 1832 when Elliot and Hill built a new instrument. This was reconstructed in 1859 by William Hill and Sons. The case remained intact, but the organ was mechanically new, retaining the largest pipes of the former instrument. In 1903, J. W. Walker and Sons built a new instrument in the same case, retaining several registers from the previous instrument. There was more work in 1918 by Harrison & Harrison when the Tuba Mirabilis was added and the great chorus revised. The same firm rebuilt this Walker-Harrison instrument in 1931 when a new console and electro-pneumatic action were added together with four new stops. The smaller solo tubas were enclosed in the solo box. Over the years there have been some aptly named organists and assistant organists: Edwin George Monk (1859), Geoffrey Coffin (1971–1975), Robert Sharpe (2008) and David Pipe (from 2010).

On 20 July 1967 York Glazier's Trust was established. It is Britain's oldest and largest specialist stained glass conservation studio, dedicated to the care and conservation of stained glass in York, York Minster (all 128 of the windows) and throughout the UK. The trust offers conservation, repair and protection of medieval stained glass, of enamel painted glass of the seventeenth century and Georgian era, of Victorian and Edwardian stained glass, of twentieth-century windows and of historic plain glazing. The trust has worked on four Oxford Colleges (Balliol, Lincoln, New College and Trinity) and many parish churches throughout England and Wales, the east window at All Saints, Porthcawl and panels from the west window of Beverley Minster.

In 1961 Frederick Donald Coggan, Baron Coggan, left his post as Bishop of Bradford to become Archbishop of York; he went on to be the 101st Archbishop of Canterbury from 1974 to 1980. 25 September 1963 saw Mrs Donald Coggan open York's first hostel for deaf girls in Bootham on the top floor of the York and District Deaf and Dumb Society. Mrs Coggan herself became deaf during a flight in the non-pressurised cabin of an aircraft in East Africa.

Politically speaking, York was Conservative until 1964 with Charles Longbottom the MP; Alex Lyon then took the seat for Labour until he lost it in 1983 to the Tories.

York City Council in session in the Guildhall in 1965. (Photo courtesy of York Press)

Municipal vandalism was still all the rage in the '60s. Among the precious historical buildings lost to us were St Mary Bishophill Senior (pre-Conquest, 1963) some of the building went to the new Church of the Holy Redeemer in Boroughbridge Road; Bedern Chapel, reduced to a ruin because of its tilt, but now happily a Grade II-listed building; The Elephant & Castle, Skeldergate; The Queen's Head, Fossgate (replaced by a flat wall); No. 4 Micklegate, which featured an early eighteenth-century staircase to make way for an extension to the drab Co-op building – now itself thankfully demolished; ditto No. 18 Micklegate and its Jacobean ceiling; St Maurice's Church, Monkgate; No. 27 Trinity Lane and its Georgian overmantel.

In Haxby, the fine building that was Haxby Hall was demolished in 1963. It was originally owned by the Wood and Hardcastle families who owed a jewellers in Stonegate, and then by the Wards. A perfectly fine building was knocked down despite local protests and replaced with the dullest construction imaginable. The original Grade II-listed building situated in twenty-two acres was built in 1790; an unusual, striking feature was the glass cupola over the stairwell. It had started life as a private residence and was used up to 1853 as the Revd John Heslop's Classical and Mathematical Academy for 'Sons of Gentlemen of high respectability; £50 per annum including washing.' Apart from the usual maths, Latin and Greek, lessons included 'Navigation, the Use of Globes, and the Construction of Maps'. In the Second World War it was requisitioned to accommodate evacuees from Hull and Middlesbrough as well as being the local first aid centre and HQ for the ARP. In 1950 Kenneth Ward, the then owner, had donated nine acres to the village which then became the Ethel Ward Memorial Playing Field in honour of his late wife and now comprises a scout hut, playground, football pitches and other facilities for the enjoyment of local residents. The field was opened in 1948 by Maurice Leyland, England and Yorkshire cricketer. Between 1961 and 1971 the population of the village expanded by 50 per cent requiring a new school to be built off Usher Lane and reflecting the rapid house-building programme going on all around York in the '60s.

Old Haxby Hall with its distinctive cupola - an unhappy example of the unnecessary destruction of a perfectly serviceable building, replaced by a piece of functional non-architecture.

The preservation and conservation of the best bits of historical York, were, of course, never left just to Lord Esher and an often reluctant and wrong-headed council. A number of organisations had long been active in fighting for preservation and conservation, and continued to be so in the '60s. We have already mentioned York's Georgian Society; it was founded in 1939 to preserve and care for Georgian buildings in and around York while encouraging their study and appreciation. It is the second oldest society outside London devoted to the Georgian era with a remit that extends beyond architecture and associated crafts to include the arts, culture and society of the period from 1660, the year of George I's birth, to 1837, the year William IV died.

In 1968 Pamela Ward, then a student at the university, organised one of the first conservation conferences ever held in the UK; it took place in King's Manor under the aegis of the Institute of Advanced Architectural Studies and attracted everyone who was anyone in the field.

York Civic Trust was founded at the Mansion House in 1946 by

four men who saw the potential dangers that could beset an historic city immediately after the war, when there was a prevailing 'spirit of renewal'. These founder members had experience in various fields including the church and commerce, but above all they had a passion for York. They intended that the trust should have a wider remit than preservation alone, and hoped it would assist in schemes to improve the amenities in the city.

The four men included the Dean of York, Oliver Sheldon of Rowntrees and J. B. Morrell.

In 1962 The Royal Commission on Historical Monuments published Volume I of its *Inventory for the City, Eboracum: Roman York* shedding invaluable light on excavated Roman and Anglian artefacts. It covered roads, military and civilian sites, burials, inscriptions, glass and other fragments of Roman York. The fourth Viking Congress was held in York in 1965.

Yorkshire Architectural & York Archaeological Society (YAYAS) had also been very active. The society was founded

> to promote the study of ecclesiastical architecture, antiquities, and design, the restoration of mutilated remains, and of churches which may be been desecrated, within the county of York: and the improvement, as far as may be within its province, of the character of ecclesiastical edifices to be erected in the future.

The first meeting was held in York on 7 October 1842. Its rather grand membership consisted of patrons: The Archbishop of York and the Bishop of Ripon; presidents, the lord's lieutenants of the three ridings; vice-presidents, local nobility, knights and Members of Parliament; and ordinary members, clergymen and lay members of the Church of England.

York Civic Trust had a busy decade; here are some of their projects:

The 1960 Festival of York was attended by Queen Elizabeth the Queen Mother, and unlike the previous festival the Mystery Plays went ahead uninterrupted by the rain.

The restoration of Walmgate Bar was completed and work was begun on the Baedeker-raid-damaged St Martin-le-Grand church in Coney Street. It was re-hallowed in April 1968 with a dedication to peace and reconciliation. There has been a clock telling us the time at St Martin's since 1668. Although nothing now remains of the original, the famous 'Little Admiral' came to life in 1779, and the decorated bracket and ornaments from 1856. Damaged in the 1942 raid, local clockmaker Geoffrey Newey built a new movement in 1966 which, like its predecessor, was housed in the tower and drives the hands by means of a series of connected rods running some 20 metres over the roof. His is one of the last traditional turret clock movements to be installed in this country. The church's website adds more:

> The 1856 clock was made to strike the hours, and in 1925 chimes were added by Geoffrey Newey's grandfather GJF Newey. The original intention was to restore these to the restored church. After the bells were stolen in about 1960 it was not clear whether this would be possible. One new bell was installed which enabled it to strike the hours; however that was quickly disconnected when the caretaker of the press works who had a flat close to the tower complained that the sound kept him awake. The bed for the new clock was also made large enough to contain a chiming mechanism, but that was never commissioned.

Application for preservation work on No. 16 Coney Street at the corner of New Street was lodged when the purchaser applied to demolish the building – formerly St Martin's Bank. The medieval timber-framed house at No. 111 Walmgate was purchased and, on completion, was named Bowes Morrell House after the trust's first chairman.

One of York's jewels – indeed, one of England's jewels – is All Saint's Church in North Street and the wonderful stained glass windows housed there. In 1961 the trust contributed to the restoration of those windows. The striking 120-foot spire is but one of this church's many treasures. Emma Raughton, a visionary anchorite, lived in an anchor hold here – a two-storey house attached to the aisle. Other marvels include a figure in one of the fourteenth-century windows wearing glasses – one of the world's earliest depictions of spectacles – and representations of the green man in the aisles and nave. The church has some of the finest medieval stained glass in Europe that is not in York Minster, including the aisle window which shows the Six Corporal Acts of Mercy (as in Matthew) and the famous 1410 Doom Window (or 'Pricke of Conscience' window) which graphically depicts your last fifteen days before the Day of Judgement. There is also an outstanding fifteenth-century hammer-beam ceiling decorated with beautiful, colourful angels.

In 1964 the trust anticipated to some extent the findings of the Esher Report when it published its *Historic Buildings – Problems of their Preservation* by June Hargreaves. It spotlighted seventeen streets and areas which the trust aimed to target, these in effect became the Conservation Areas required by the government in the 1967 Civic Amenities Act. Parts of the King's Manor were restored and a ceiling from a Tudor House in North Street dating from *c.* 1600 was salvaged and transferred to a room in King's Manor. The issue of traffic versus preservation was ever-present and, in the light of the Buchanan Report on Traffic in Towns, the trust reasserted its concerns over 'the voracious appetite of the motor car' and its pains to avoid 'the Minster sitting in the middle of a gigantic car park'. Extensive traffic-free precincts, with adequate car parks around the walls, was the solution. Thirty years later this finally became a reality.

John Betjeman visited churches and York museums that year and admitted it to be 'one of the best days I can recall in a long life'. His parting words were: 'Sun on grass and stone and brick, evensong in the Minster, gin in the William IV!' Redundant churches and their productive reuse, and the commercial, recreational and aesthetic potential of the River Ouse were examined, the latter in the River Ouse Survey Report published in 1965.

That same year the splendid Fairfax House started to emerge from the shadows of dilapidation when it was bought by the council. It is, by common consent, one of the finest Georgian town houses in England. Fairfax House was originally the winter home of Viscount Fairfax, having been purchased in 1760 as a dowry to Anne Fairfax. Its richly decorated interior was redesigned in the classical style by York architect John Carr with its magnificent staircase, ceilings, Venetian window and iron balusters. Adapted in the last century for use as a cinema and dance hall, Fairfax House was restored to its former glory by York Civic Trust in 1982/84. Sir Simon Jenkins said of it in 2003, 'it is the most perfect eighteenth-century townhouse I have come across anywhere in England.' The Noel Terry collection of furniture, clocks, paintings and decorative arts, described by Christie's as one of the finest private collections of the twentieth century, elegantly furnish the house.

At the other end of the spectrum, 1965 was the year in which the trust was compelled to lament the council's erection of Stonebow and the emasculation of St Saviourgate. They described it as 'an uninspiring hotchpotch of the mediocre, culminating in

Above: Stonebow in 1963. (Photo courtesy of York Press)

Right: The Salem Chapel in St Saviourgate before it was torn down in the '60s. After its demolition a 'refugee camp' was set up on the site. Not a real one but a demonstration of the conditions in which refugees lived.

Stonebow House' which had 'killed' St Saviour's church and St Saviourgate 'and shuddered to think what it would look like when its rough concrete started to weather'. Now we know. And the trust asked why?

The appointment in 1966 of Lord Esher as consultant was seen as a 'watershed in the history of both the Trust and the City'. In 1967 brewers J. W. Cameron of West Hartlepool (now Hartlepool) presented the trust with Nos 17–19 Aldwark, 'an architectural plum pudding with all sorts of good things inside it'. The house was restored and renovated and was named Oliver Sheldon House after another of the trust's four founders. It had originally, from 1820, been the home of the Croft family, importers of port. John Croft was described in the deeds as a 'Merchant of Apporto'. Sir John Hunt, of John J. Hunt who owned the Ebor Brewery in York, had lived there since 1937.

A landmark decision was made that year when the owner of No. 22 Stonegate applied for permission to demolish the building, in the face of opposition from the council and the trust he was refused by the Minister who applied a Building Preservation Order on the grounds that the preservation of the integrity of Stonegate was in the public interest. Had the application been allowed then the floodgates surely would have opened and sites less impressive than Stonegate would have been vulnerable.

An application was sent to the Redundant Churches Commission to convert the church of St Mary in Castlegate as a home for a permanent exhibition of York's history; the result was The York Story which opened in 1972 after fourteen years of dereliction. It closed in 2001. Its spire is the tallest in the city. This Grade II-listed church, which was de-consecrated in 1958, has been home to a contemporary visual arts venue since 2004. The vexed question of traffic snarling around the Minster along Deangate was raised again and the trust found its first permanent home in Walmgate – at Bowes Morrell House.

Trainspotting was one of the things to do, especially for boys, in the '60s.

1968 saw the restoration of an often overlooked treasure in the yard of No. 52 Stonegate. It is the oldest domestic building in York and was very large, obviously owned by a man of some wealth and taste. It is the only surviving example in York of Norman domestic stonework in its original location. This house was built between 1170 and 1180 when the wealthy were building in stone on a scale unseen before: stone meant status. The fact that it was a house is revealed by the fact that the windows were unglazed. Instead of glass, the inhabitants used shutters with a metal bar across for safety. Also, archaeologists found a medieval toilet on the site.

The History of York website tells us that 'originally there would have been a large hall on the first floor which would have been used as living quarters. You can see where the floor level was in the line of red stone that remains on the right hand wall. An undercroft below would have been used for storage'.

In 1969 the trust supported the government's plan to establish the National Railway Museum in York. Stonegate was finally closed to traffic. The old Roman stone paving – hence the name – survives under the cobbles, complete with the central gulley for the chariots' skid wheels. It was the Roman *via praetoria*. Queen Mary, wife of George V, when living at Goldsborough Hall near Knaresborough, was a frequent shopper here in the 1920s and '30s. Unfortunately for the shop owners she was a devotee of 'honouring', the practice whereby patronage alone was considered sufficient payment for the goods she left the shops with.

The reintroduction of swans on the River Ouse was mooted by the Trust; two pairs were donated to the city by the Worshipful Company of Dyers – responsible for swans on the Thames.

Other preservation and conservation projects in the '60s included the restoration of John Carr's Assize Court building in the eye of York, the restoration of More House in Heslington and its conversion into the Catholic Chaplaincy serving the university, staffed by clergy from Ampleforth Abbey. More House had been the vicarage for St Paul's, the parish church at Heslington. In 1967 the Theatre Royal received a 'brilliant reconstruction' making it 'unexpectedly the best piece of modern architecture in York', according to Patrick Nuttgens in his *City Buildings: York*. In 1961 lightning miraculously missed the Minster and struck the diminutive by comparison Boer War Memorial instead.

The Cold War bunker was York's worst kept secret. Opened in 1961, this piece of Cold War furniture was officially No. 20 Group Royal Observer HQ operated by UKWMO, the UK Warning and Monitoring Organisation. Its role was to function as one of the UK's twenty-nine monitoring and listening posts in the event of a nuclear explosion. Decommissioned in 1991, English Heritage have opened it to the public to enable them to see the decontamination areas, living quarters, a communications centre and operations rooms.

In 1968 the last of four phases in the College of Further Education was completed at Dringhouses, as were buildings at Askham Bryan College of Agriculture. Half Moon Court was opened at the wonderful Castle Museum in 1963 as a reconstruction of a street around the end of the First World War. That same year the more functional York Crematorium was completed, reflecting Asplund's famous crematorium in Stockholm. Bootham School's 500-seater assembly hall was completed in 1966, winner of the RIBA award for Yorkshire.

Bootham's new hall under construction in 1965.

In 1968 the Folk Hall in New Earswick was refurbished and included a new swimming pool. The hall was built in 1907 at a cost of £2,278 15s 11/2d. Joseph Rowntree, whose brainchild it was, actively encouraged women to get out of the home and use the many facilities offered there: 'In this country it seems to be the thought that women do not need recreation' he pondered, citing the example of Germany, where it was and still is the norm for families to go out together as families, with the children. During the First World War the hall was used to shelter Belgian refugees. The village library was here from 1908, with the first 100 books donated by Joseph Rowntree. Many social activities were held in the Folk Hall – one of the purposes of which was to offer societies and clubs a place in which to run activities, reflecting the interests of the residents. In the late '40s the hall took 1,075 lettings in one year, bringing in £710 with highly profitable Saturday night dances proving particularly popular. The same year, the North Eastern Electricity Board Centre was completed in Hungate, as was the tavern in the town on Ouse Bridge – a former brewery and then a pub exhibiting features of many different periods, replete with paraphernalia. An obtrusive eight-story 'slab block on a podium' (Nuttgens) blotted the Ouse landscape as the Viking Hotel.

Hotel Slab on the Ouse.

Chapter 3

Streets, Squares, Gardens and Gates, Bars, Bridges and Rivers

The Esher Report sheds important and interesting light on what some of the streets of York were like in the '60s: 'The effect of the new market place with its delightful backdrop of the restored backs of the Shambles, is totally ruined by the enormous backside of Marks & Spencer's, which has gone far to spoil a carefully handled and public-spirited enterprise'.

Piccadilly: '… this notorious example of twentieth century non-architecture'.

Chapter House Street: '… for variety of colour and texture, subtle juxtaposition of small elements and sudden contrast of small with great, this is unexcelled anywhere in England'.

In the '60s the effect of opening up Deangate from Goodramgate in 1903 was clearly felt: 'its effect has been unfortunate, almost disastrous. For its existence has meant that the route … has become a main route, taking through as well as city traffic. The precinctual effect of the surroundings of the Minster has been shattered'.

Coffee Yard: 'One of the most alluring of York's alleyways … then into a delightful small courtyard … emerging into Stonegate in its central, most handsome part'.

Goodramgate: '… still one of the most attractive streets in York, even though it has suffered a brutal intrusion recently … the buildings are nearly all two-storey or low three-story, with one excrescence, the Hunter & Smallpage building … [Goodramgate's] hidden gem is Holy Trinity Church, behind 'Lady Row' … the disastrous new building [is opposite] of gross scale … monstrously out of sympathy with everything else in the street'.

The '60s in Goodramgate witnessed much demolition. Shaw's wet fish shop, Welburn's tobacconists and Steigmann's pork butchers – opposite the Cross Keys – were all knocked down to be replaced by a nondescript building housing the Fine Fare supermarket. Opposite the delightful Holy Trinity church the Albany Ballroom, Benson's bike shop and Wilson's gun shop were all demolished with the gap serving as a derelict car park until the 1980s.

In King's Square and King's Court the Grapes Inn and Duke's fish shop breathed their last in the '60s and houses were knocked down in St Andrewgate. If anywhere started to reflect the growing taste for exotic foreign food in the '60s it was Goodramgate: Stanley Foo opened a Chinese restaurant (Stanley's) to go with his already established

Two views of Goodramgate in 1960 and 1963.
(Photos courtesy of York Press)

Goodramgate as Car Park.

laundry, Giovanni's Italian restaurant opened next to Hunter & Smallpage and an Indian restaurant moved into the premises vacated by Lund's the grocers. The National Trust opened their shop and café on the corner of College Street where Thomson's grocery shop once was. Hunter & Smallpage bought factory premises in Foss Islands Road in 1966.

Micklegate: 'One of the two or three finest streets in York ... broad and dignified – its character is dominantly, though not wholly, Georgian ... in a grander manner than any other of the inter-mural streets of York'.

Museum Gardens: 'One of the most beautiful city parks in England ... late Georgian picturesque landscaping, and their focal points are the Museum in the serenely Grecian style and the contrasting romantic ruins of St Mary's Abbey'.

In the 1960s St Helen's Square 'is now unfortunately a busy traffic intersection, not improved visually by the frigidly symmetrical "islands" in the middle'.

St Leonard's Place and Exhibition Square was recognised in the '60s as potentially one of the city's best townscapes, sadly it is still not realised: 'The only piece of town-planning in the Regency tradition in York ... the stucco crescent is a handsome composition ... the delightful King's Manor buildings ... the Victorian art Gallery with its ugly but appropriate façade ... the fine early Victorian stucco De Grey Rooms, the gloomy Gothic Theatre Royal ... this is potentially one of the best townscapes in York'.

St Saviourgate: 'A sad example of a very attractive York street which has suffered serious architectural assaults in the last few years ... it was something of an architectural oasis'.

Skeldergate: 'Has one of the most crudely designed minor buildings in York, a new public house with "wavy" boarding as on a garden shed, a sort of parody of the traditional straight weatherboarding of Essex or Kent'.

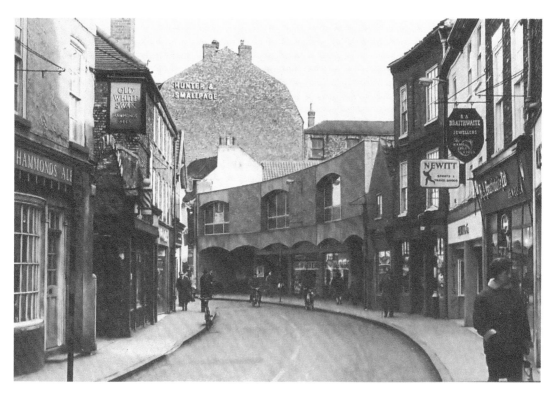

Above: Hunter & Smallpage in the '60s.
(Photo courtesy of York Press)

Right: King's Square in 1960. (Photo
courtesy of York Press)

St Saviourgate in 1961. (Photo courtesy of York Press)

Keeping your head down passing under Skekdergate Bridge on a flooded Ouse. No sign of health and safety here in 1963. (Photo courtesy of York Press)

In 1967 a 'roomy end terrace family home with five bedrooms off Bishopthorpe Road' was on the market for £2,800.

On 28 October 1963, the temporary bridge over the Ouse built by the British Army to cope with the extra traffic generated by the wedding of Duke and Duchess of Kent at York Minster was replaced by a permanent bridge. 4,000 tons of concrete and 50 tons of reinforced steel were used.

In the 1960s the demise of the rivers Ouse and Foss as commercial arteries was well established. Within the city walls only eight firms still used the rivers: Herald Printers brought in 50 tons or so of newsprint by barge once a month, Rowntrees had three or four barges per year going into their bonded warehouse and one a week as tenants into the Corporation's warehouse and Stewart Esplen & Co. brought in dried fruit every day. On the Foss, Walkers still dredged as far as Naburn collecting 150 tons of builders' sand in the process; the Power Station used the water for cooling.

On the recreational side, two companies operated between them eight launches and twenty skiffs from below Lendal Bridge and South Esplanade. The 138 members of the York Motor Boat Club made use of the Ouse as did the Rowing Club who shared their boathouse at Lendal Bridge with the university. The boys at St Peter's also rowed there. The Rowing Club held two regattas every year. The terrace of the Museum Gardens was the favoured place for anglers. Because there was a 15s lock charge on the Foss, there was little activity on that river.

The Esher Report had a decidedly romantic view of the Ouse: 'Looking downstream from Lendal, beyond the wooden landing stages, the middle distance is almost Venetian, with Gothic and neo-Gothic architecture rising straight out of the water'.

On 2 January 1961, the Yorkshire Museum and the Museum Gardens were given in trust to York City Council by Yorkshire Philosophical Society. It was not long before the society had a fight on its hands as the Corporation decided to knock down part of the abbey walls in Exhibition Square – including St Margaret's Arch – and relocate it elsewhere. A roundabout would then be built at the junction of Bootham to improve traffic flow. This intended act of vandalism was defeated, largely with the help of the society and a timely reminder of an 1896 legal agreement forbidding destruction or removal of the abbey walls.

The Philosophical Society was founded in 1822 by four York gentlemen: William Salmond (1769–1838) a retired colonel and amateur geologist, Anthony Thorpe (1759–1829), James Atkinson (1759–1839) a retired surgeon, and William Vernon (1789–1871) son of Archbishop Vernon of York, Vicar of Bishopthorpe. The first three met for the first minuted meeting of the society on 7 December 1822. Their aim was to collect together and house their collections of fossil bones, which had recently been discovered at Kirkdale Cave. Vernon attended the second meeting on 14 December, at which the prospectus was drawn up 'to establish at York, a philosophical society, and to form a scientific library and a museum'. Vernon went on to become president. The society's name comes from the days when 'natural philosopher' was the term for a scientist. The museum was founded by the Yorkshire Philosophical Society to display their geological and archaeological collections. It was in Ousegate until 1828 when the society received, by royal grant, ten acres of land from St Mary's Abbey in

Temporary bridge and completed Clifton Bridge. (Photos courtesy of York Press)

King's Staith in 1964. (Photo courtesy of York Press)

order to build a new museum. The main building was designed by William Wilkins in Greek Revival style and was officially opened in February 1830, making it one of the oldest established museums in England. A condition of the royal grant was that the surrounding land should become a botanical garden. This was completed in the 1830s, as the Museum Gardens. Now known as the British Science Association, the British Association for the Advancement of Science was founded with the help of the Yorkshire Philosophical Society and held its inaugural meeting at the Yorkshire Museum in 1831. In 1969 the society published an illustrated article on the history of the swimming bath along with their usual scientific, academic papers.

Chapter 4

Going Out in York

On 27 November 1963 The Beatles played at the Rialto Theatre. There had been earlier Beatles concerts there on 27 February, 13 March and 29 May that year. The November set list comprised ten songs including 'She Loves You', 'Boys', and 'Till There Was You'. For the March gig John Lennon was unable to perform due to illness, so The Beatles performed as a three-piece – the only time they ever did that. In February Helen Shapiro, the headline act, was ill with flu for a second consecutive day, and so didn't perform. George Harrison told Stacy Brewer of the *Yorkshire Evening Press* that after the February concert the group wrote their next single 'From Me to You' on the tour bus journey from York to the next gig in Shrewsbury. Their third concert at the Rialto was part of the Beatles' UK tour with Roy Orbison.

Paul McCartney signing autographs outside The Rialto.

The Rolling Stones played two sets at the Rialto on 26 February 1964. Members of the band signed their names in lipstick on the wall of the top floor bar in Peter Madden's bar (now Plunkett's) in 1968 after a concert in Leeds. The Rialto was a marvellous 1930s art deco cinema and a concert venue hosting such legends as Louis Armstrong, Sarah Vaughan, Jerry Lee Lewis, Count Basie and, of course, The Beatles. The myopic council saw fit to demolish it in 2003 to make way for a Mecca bingo hall car park. The owner, Jack Prendergast, had a son who was projectionist there. He had aspirations to musicianship and took organ lessons from Francis Jackson at the Minster. That son was John Barry who went on to form the John Barry Seven and score many a Bond theme, *Midnight Cowboy*, *Out of Africa* and *Born Free*.

In 1961 Prendergast sold the Rialto to Mecca and in April 1962 Helen Shapiro appeared, but this scoop – like many others at the time – was no thanks to Mecca. Don McCallion the manager there used to hire the Mecca and put on and promote his own shows.

In November 1964 P. J. Proby, the Pretty Things and the Barron Knights were billed to perform but Proby had to pull out due to 'appearance difficulties'. Chuck Berry stood in and trousered his fee. Mecca's Eric Morley announced the building of a £4 million complex behind the Mecca in Fishergate accommodating 2,000 people and 300 cars. It opened as Tiffany's in 1966 but closed eight months later, reopening in late 1967 as the Cat's Whiskers for dining, dancing and cabaret. The Heartbeat Discotheque opened there in 1969, 'York's most luxurious In Place'. Hypnotique hypnotised you in Lady Peckett's Yard; Old World kept going round and round in Stonegate; while Jack & Jill's were in Bootham, Brummells were in Middlethorpe Hall and Intercom in Stonebow House.

Super Sixties week at Clifton Green Primary School: Years 3–6 did a '60s themed week which produced some fabulous outfits and work on the decade.

York had not escaped the craze for skiffle. In 1958 the Columba Club in Sir Thomas Herbert's House was Friday night host to the Planets, comprising one thirteen year old and four fourteen year olds, all from St Michael's College in Leeds. Youth clubs closed at 9.30 p.m. and at weekends and there was nothing much in the dance halls for younger people, until, that is, Father John Murphy opened his beat club in his Our Lady's church in Acomb in 1963. Neil Guppy was the trendsetter though; from 1961 he started the Enterprise Club and put on jive parties at Clifton Cinema Ballroom on Fridays, and at the Woolpack in Peasholme Green on Wednesdays and Saturdays in Acomb Church Hall and in Betty's Bar. By 1966, twenty-seven-year-old Neil had 1,500 members and gave up his teaching post to concentrate on his evening job. The Enterprise Club was in Walmgate by 1966.

York also had its own home-grown music scene with venues like the Kavern Club in Micklegate, the Mandrake in Stonegate, and Neil Guppy's Enterprise Club hosting live music by young city bands. Some of it started in the '50s, but much of it persisted throughout the '60s or originated in that decade. The Kavern Club started life as a coffee bar, it was in the basement of the Labour Party headquarters, appropriately decorated with graffiti. By 1964 there were 100 or so local groups performing in the city: allegedly the crime rate fell because most young people were either performing in groups or watching them.

The Kavern Club in Micklegate in 1964. (Photo Courtesy of York Press)

When psychedelia became cool, York's main protagonists were Roll Movement, Angel Pavement, and the Smoke. Roll Movement supported names like Cream, the Who and Pink Floyd.

In September 1964 the York Theatre Royal made a valiant attempt to get in on the act, booking the Merseybeats and Little Eva. Sadly it came to nothing when the Merseybeats, 'exhausted from the strain of touring', cancelled. That same summer, the *Evening Press* was reporting 'a beat group's boom in York', but more bad luck was to ensue. The much vaunted Attic club in Clifford Street, destined to be run by teenagers, hit financial problems in 1965 before it opened and the Pretty Things were very late for their Zarf Club gig in Stonegate after a crash involving the van carrying their instruments. Local group Gideon's Few stood in for them and loaned them their kit. It was Gideon's Few who played a record breaking ten-hour marathon set non-stop in the Zarf Club in September 1965.

In late 1966 the visionary management of the Tin Chicken Club at New Earswick's Folk Hall booked a band called The Paramounts to play at one of their regular Saturday night concerts some months down the line. Just before the gig in 1967 The Paramounts released a single called A Whiter Shade of Pale and changed their name to the Faux Latin Procol Harum. The Move, Pink Floyd and Ike and Tina Turner are said to have played there as well.

According to the *Evening Press*, folk music enjoyed something of a revival in the decade. Eight students from St John's formed the popular Garden Street Philharmonia International, breaking up in 1965 but reforming to perform on Opportunity Knocks. Neil Guppy ran folk nights at his Enterprise Club in Dixon's Yard, Walmgate. York Folk Festival was held in 1968, while the always packed Lowther was home to the York Folk Club, bringing in artists such as Al Stewart.

Jazz, of course, started off in the '50s at the York Jazz Club in the dance studios in High Ousegate, later becoming the Studio Club. In 1958 the Jazz Attic Club opened on the top floor of a house in Petergate above Pete Madden's restaurant. In 1955 nine local schoolboys formed a band but had to remain anonymous in the press as their school was anti-group and considered jazz 'unsuitable'. The Empire Jazz club opened in 1959. Jazz could also be heard in the Clifton Ballroom and nearby at the Burton Stone Inn. 1963 saw the opening of York Jazz Scene in Acomb Church Hall. Bobby Hirst organised a significant concert of modern jazz in the Tempest Anderson Hall at the Yorkshire Museum followed in 1966 by another big jazz concert in St George's Hall.

The jukebox had a difficult birth in York, perhaps not totally surprising if you consider that the origin of the word jukebox came into use in the United States in 1940, derived from the familiar usage juke joint, itself derived from the Gullah word 'juke' or 'joog' meaning disorderly, rowdy, or wicked. Gullah are descendants of enslaved Africans who live in South Carolina and Georgia. Anyway, when the Golden Fleece in Pavement and the White Swan in Goodramgate each applied for a license to install one, York's Chief Constable refused, describing them as 'unsuitable and undesirable instruments to have in a public house bar or lounge'. Drinking yourself stupid was fine though. The concern also was that the landlord had no control of the choice of music selected and that a random injudicious choice of disc may annoy other customers. On the other hand, record players or radiograms were permitted in five other pubs, and the Licensing Justices allowed a special case for York Empire in 1959 when the owners sagely pointed out that the absence of a jukebox would drive youngsters onto the streets where hooliganism would surely ensue. In the same year the Justices spitefully imposed restrictions on the numbers at dances in dance halls. The Empire was pegged to 600, Christie's Ballroom in Clarence Street was restricted to 650 and the Assembly Rooms to 500. The Railway Institute gymnasium was permitted 1,400 for dances and 2,000 for seated events.

To meet the obvious demand, dance schools proliferated in the city before and throughout the '60s. The Central School of Dancing in High Ousegate was famous, in 1955 the Court School of Dancing opened in the same venue, in the '60s Saturday teenage classes were hugely popular with up to 300 turning up at any one time. The Regency School of Dancing was next to St George's cinema in Castlegate from 1956 and in 1964 they held the Dance of the Season in what was then the Regency Dance Studio. MacPherson's Dance School was in Bishophill run by Mary Mac.

In York the twist was highly controversial. A number of dance schools regarded it as 'vulgar and tribal', banning it because it attracted 'the sort of students we did not want'. One teacher sneered that movements required for stubbing out a cigarette end on the floor gave you everything you needed to perfect the twist, apparently. The New Earswick Bop for a Bob persisted with the jive but the twist gradually won through, led by the Empire.

Popular record shops started opening in 1959. In Bridge Street Mackenzie's styled itself as 'York's only record browserie for pops, jazz and classical records, players and grams' – the first self-service record shop outside London with its iconic record hoods and 'any record any artist available'. In 1955 Hugh Robertson opened his shop in Acomb selling records, sheet music, portable record players and gramophones. Banks was in Lendal, and still is, although now selling mainly classical. It was founded in 1756 and shares its birthday with Mozart. If you wanted a top of the range deck you had to go to the nearest Comet, in Leeds.

Pamela Ward, one of the contributors to the 1968 Esher Report, described nightlife in York in the mid-sixties in an appendix to the report:

> The city apparently dies at night; pleasures are not highbrow, and tend to finish early; in contrast to the Minster and Georgian streets, the majority of people, workers in the traditional industries, chocolate and railways included, traders and their premises, are unassuming, unpretentious, small scale, in fact still medieval – a gentle way of saying that once you live in it York no longer retains, except in certain lights at certain times, the dignified aura of an historic city of international significance. It is a scruffy, friendly, blunt, unambitious place and lacks the 'culture' and intellectual consciousness one might expect. If its fabric has lasted this long, it is probably the work of a few keen individuals, similar to those who fight for it today, rather than of the unseeing and apathetic affection of the man in the street.

Plus ça change.

A quick pint after work, particularly on Fridays, was a popular and, for many, an essential event. An article in the 1960s student magazine, *Eboracum*, described a typical night out:

> The White Horse and The Market Tavern, The Lendal Bridge, The Coach & Horses, and others, are at weekends packed to capacity with young people from York and the villages outside, flash girls, farm workers, hard men and rockers. The rock pubs are all things to all men. A rumble is the easiest. An air of frustrated violence fills the already crowded bars and a spilled drink, a casual glance at an unknown girl, a 'joke' is enough excuse for a fight. Walking down Coppergate between eleven and twelve on a Saturday night can be frightening and, occasionally, dangerous.

Micklegate was ever rowdy while the more discerning drank in the two pubs in Stonegate or in Youngs.

York Theatre Royal thrived through the '60s. The first theatre in York was built on tennis courts in Minster Yard in 1734 by Thomas Keregan. In 1744, his widow built the New Theatre on the site of what was the city's mint – itself built on the site of St Leonard's Hospital. In 1765 it was rebuilt and enlarged to seat 550; access to the site of the mint can still be gained from the back of the main stage. At that time, the theatre was illegal and it was not until a royal patent was granted in 1769 that this status changed. The theatre was renamed the Theatre Royal. Gas lighting was introduced in 1824 and in 1835 a new frontage was built, facing onto the newly created St Leonard's Place. York Theatre Royal's stage was rebuilt to include traps and in 1875 substantial renovations included stage boxes, upholstered seats in the dress circle, the construction of the upper circle, the rebuilding of the gallery, the renovation of the proscenium arch and the enlargement

A 1969 Theatre Royal Production of
A Christmas Carol. (Photo courtesy
of York Press)

of the pit. Five years later, a new Victorian Gothic frontage was added, decorated with carved heads representing Elizabeth I and characters from Shakespeare. In 1888, the area beneath the dress circle was opened out to extend the pit (today's stalls), giving the theatre a capacity of 1400. A further reconstruction took place in 1967 with York Theatre Royal's new front-of-house facilities and a staircase in the award-winning concrete-and-glass foyer extension. The Theatre Royal did some Shakespeare and lots of Pinter and Wesker. Special productions were put on for students but they preferred less highbrow stuff like *Dracula* and *Love or Money*, a comedy thriller.

The basement of the De Grey Rooms housed the original kitchens, cold rooms, wine cellars and storage facilities. The Oak Room, previously the kitchen, spent the 1950s and '60s as a restaurant.

The Grand Opera House became a theatre almost by accident. The buildings in which it exists today were originally constructed as the city's Corn Exchange in 1868, the intention being to use it as a concert hall on an ad hoc basis. The auditorium was a warehouse opening on King Street. William Peacock converted the Corn Exchange into the Grand Opera House and opened on 20 January 1902 with *Little Red Riding Hood*, starring Florrie Ford. In 1903 it had a subtle but important change of name to 'the Grand Opera House and Empire' so that regulations banning smoking in theatres could be circumvented – the then fashionable habit of smoking was permitted in music halls. It began to present 'varieties' in order to avoid direct competition with the Theatre Royal. The Grand Opera House stayed with William Peacock's family until 1945, providing a varied programme that included pantomime, music hall, variety, serious

The Grand Opera House in the '60s. (Photo courtesy of York Press)

theatre, amateur opera, plays, revues, and silent films. Performers included Charlie and Sydney Chaplin, Gracie Fields, Lillie Langtry, George Robey, Cecily Courtneidge and Jimmy Jewel. In 1945–56, F. J. Butterworth owned the theatre and stars such as Vera Lynn, Laurel and Hardy and Morecambe and Wise appeared. The theatre was closed in 1956, bought by Ernest Shepherd of the Shambles, and reopened as the S. S. Empire (Shepherd of Shambles) in 1958 for roller skating and dancing, which ran throughout the '60s. In September 1967 *Lock Up Your Daughters* was showing.

When the Empire closed in 1956 a sign went up on the wall exclaiming, 'This theatre has been closed by the crippling Entertainment Tax and unfair untaxed entertainment by television. Television pays no tax, television presents music-hall shows seven days a week including Sundays – the theatre is not allowed to open on Sunday. Losses sustained by television are made up out of your – the taxpayer's – pocket. No other business in the country could survive under such deliberately unfair competition. Where is British fair-play?' This chimed with a period of decline in theatres and cinemas, which wasn't reversed until the 1980s.

The flamboyant Hans Hess was curator at the York City Art Gallery from 1947 until 1954 when he took over as York Festival Director, the festival second only in reputation to the Edinburgh Festival; before that he was heavily involved in the revival of the festival in 1951. Having brought the art gallery into the 20th century – he was a friend of Kandinsky, Klee and Feininger and his gallery Visitors' Book sold for a very handsome sum at auction – Hess set to work on resuscitating the York Festival until his departure for Sussex University as Reader in Art History in 1966. His uncompromising stand on standards in art, his criticism of arts funding and his Marxist politics (probably all a bit much for an artistically pedestrian York at the time), earned him the rancour of the local press and probably accounted for a right-wing arson attack on his house. To put his contribution to York art and culture into perspective, Patrick Nuttgens, in his *History of York*, says of him: 'To Hess York owes the biggest cultural impetus in the 20th century until the arrival of the University'.

The wonderful painting of Clifford's Tower by James Lloyd (1905–1974) which hangs in the newly refurbished City Art Gallery; it was the winner of the 1962 Evelyn award. Lloyd was a cowman at Skirpenbeck near York when he took up painting. The idea for the multitude of dots came from the grainy half-tone pictures in newspapers. (Photo courtesy of York Museums Trust)

In the early twentieth century 'animated pictures' joined variety as a competition to the Theatre Royal. Film shows were put on in the Opera House, the Festival Concert Rooms, the Exhibition Buildings, the Victoria Hall in Goodramgate, the New Street Wesleyan Chapel, and in the Theatre Royal itself. The New Street Chapel, after it ceased to be used for worship in 1908, became first the Hippodrome, and then, in 1920, the Tower Cinema, which closed in 1966; the Victoria Hall later became the National Picture Theatre but was closed for conversion to a dance hall in 1924 and later demolished. Films were also shown at the City Palace, Fishergate, which was also staging variety concerts as early as 1910; as the Rialto, it was burnt down in 1935 but was replaced by the new Rialto on the same site, rebuilt with extra-large seats. The Rialto also staged variety shows and concerts, and was still going in the 1960s. On 4 September 1967 the Regal was showing the X-certificate *You're a Big Boy Now* while at the Odeon the following day you could see a trailer for Laurence Olivier's *Henry V* (U-certificate) in technicolour. A seat in the stalls would cost you 5s, up in the circle 8s 6d.

The first building to be purpose-built as a cinema, the excitingly named The Electric, Fossgate, was opened in 1911; renamed the Scala in 1951, it was sold for use as a furniture shop in 1957. Three more cinemas opened in the next ten years: the Picture House, Coney Street, was opened in 1915 and converted to shops in 1955; The Grand, Clarence Street, opened its doors as a cinema and ballroom in 1919 but converted to a roller skating rink and ballroom in 1958; and the St George's Hall, Castlegate, was opened in 1921 and was still going in the '60s.

Fossgate in 1960 showing the furniture shop, formerly The Electric.

Four new cinemas had opened in the 1930s: the Regent, Acomb, in 1934; the art deco Odeon, Blossom Street; the Regal, Piccadilly, and the art deco Clifton in 1937. In July 1947 York voted for Sunday opening of cinemas. The peak year for attendances was 1949, when almost 60 per cent of the city's population went to the pictures. The Regent closed in 1959, but the others were still open in the '60s. Of course, none of them ever showed any good films, according to York residents. The City Film Society tried to compensate but three cinemas had closed in recent years – one ceding to bingo. Bingo reigned too at the King Street Hall in-between bouts of wrestling – women conspicuous at both; there were dog shows on Saturdays.

Classical concerts were held in the Guildhall and at Tempest Anderson Hall next to the Yorkshire Museum and, of course, at the Sir Jack Lyons Concert Hall at the university. *Life Cycle: A Cantata for Young People* by York's Emeritus Professor of Music, Wilfrid Mellors, was performed at the opening ceremony.

York Races has been a major summer event in the city for hundreds of years. Held at the Knavesmire, the races are a significant event in the nation's racing calendar. A major improvement scheme, launched in 1962, led to the opening of the magnificent six-tier grandstand in 1965. Horse races have been run at York since the reign of Roman Emperor Septimius Severus (r. AD 193–AD 211). In 1607; racing is known to have taken place on the frozen river Ouse, between Micklegate Tower and Skeldergate Postern. The first records of a race meeting are from 1709, when efforts were made to

St George's cinema in 1965. (Photo courtesy of York Press)

The Tower before and after demolition in 1966.
(Photo courtesy of York Press)

Sixties parking at York races.

improve the flood-prone course at Clifton Ings; all to no avail, so in 1730 racing moved to Knavesmire, where today's course remains. York architect, John Carr, designed and built the first Grandstand in 1754. At one August meeting in the '60s, special efforts appear to have been made to improve the catering: prodigious quantities of beef, pork and lamb were loaded into the County Stand with 400 grouse; 350 chickens; 100 Norfolk ducklings; 5000 pounds of Scotch salmon; 500 dover soles; 400 lobsters and fifty pounds of smoked salmon.

In the 1960s, Lester Piggott won the prestigious Gimcrack Stakes, in 1963, 1965, and 1967 on Talahasse, Young Emperor and Petingo respectively. He rode a winner (Die Hard) in the 1961 Ebor Handicap, and on Pandofell and Aunt Edith in the 1961 and 1966 Yorkshire Cup. In 1960 and 1964 he rode St Paddy and Sweet Moss to victory in the Dante Stakes and Matatina, Caterina, and Tower Walk in the 1963, 1966 and 1969 Nunthorpe Sweep Stakes.

Within the city walls there were three working men's clubs – thirty around the city as a whole. They were St Clement's in Queen Victoria Street, Vickers Instruments in Bishophill and York British Legion at 61 Micklegate. Down the road a maximum of forty people at any one time were allowed in The 55 Club for drinking and gambling in a Georgian ambience. The Old World Club opened in Stonegate in the wake of the failed Raceways club with gaming, dining and dancing in the basement. Tiffany's toyed with their menu and moved upmarket from the Wimpy-type menus. The Society Club in Bootham was deemed the best place to eat, with 'other facilities' for members in other rooms. What would neighbours Rowntrees have thought?

Apart from their prestigious St Helen's Square restaurant, outside catering was big business for Terry's, with functions-catering for Bird's Eye in the Assembly Rooms, the Lord Mayor's parties in nearby Mansion House, breakfasts for the legal guests at

THE MANSION HOUSE, YORK

The Mansion House.

the Judges' Lodgings round the back, and dinners at the Merchant Taylor's Hall. Queen Elizabeth was entertained twice and the Duke of Kent once at the Mansion House. One early 1960s Assembly Room lunch involved 380 vegetarian meals, including food for ten vegans – all very new then. Hunt balls and army functions for officers and their wives from Catterick were frequent and at one Tadcaster Hunt Ball the guests reputedly included Christine Keeler, Mandy Rice Davies and John Profumo, sixties scandal superstars.

The Impress Service arrived in York on 18 January 1777 'to beat up for volunteers'. So angry were sections of the community that a letter was soon sent to the Lord Mayor threatening to burn down the Mansion House if the gang was not expelled. A reward of 100 guineas was offered for conviction of the author or authors of the missive and a twelve-man guard was put on the Mansion House.

Generally, and despite the very best efforts of some of the smaller venues, York was notable for its lack of good food and entertainment – a problem which persisted into the '90s, although entertainment is still decidedly patchy and well below par compared to that on offer in similar types of city and cities of a comparable population. Then, as now, a certain arrogance seemed to prevail, with promoters and the council taking the view that York was, and is, far too good for 'that sort of thing', or worse still, 'cultured enough'.

Katharine, Duchess of Kent GCVO is the wife of Prince Edward, Duke of Kent, who is a grandson of George V and Queen Mary, and first cousin of Elizabeth II. On 8 June 1961, she married Prince Edward, Duke of Kent, at York Minster. The Duchess worked as a music teacher in Wansbeck Primary School in Hull for thirteen years. She is a direct descendant of Oliver Cromwell.

The 1961 Royal Wedding in York Minster. (Photo courtesy of York Press)

If public bathing can be regarded as entertainment then the St George's Baths were still popular in the '60s at St George's Field – the Corporation Baths. These were most popular in the winter when the outdoor Yearsley Baths proved too cold for many. York City FC remained popular in the '60s.

St George's Baths – note the Rolls-Royce in the car park. (Photo courtesy of York Press)

Clearing the snow from the terraces at Bootham Crescent. (Photo courtesy of York Press)

Chapter 5

York Working and York Shopping

It is often said that York missed out on the Industrial Revolution, reasons being, for example, that the city was too far from the sea to be an efficient port, coal was relatively expensive until the arrival of the railways, and that the city lay on flat land so did not have powerful rivers to drive water- and steam-based machinery. But be careful what you wish for, even if it be in retrospect or with hindsight. Had York been part of the revolution then we would not today have the York we have, and enjoy. Industrialisation would have left an indelible mark on the city, quite probably at the expense of some, at least, of what the city gloried in the '60s, and indeed, still glories in today.

A consequence of the industrial revolution bypass was the no-show of immigrant workers who came to other parts of Yorkshire to work the textile and steel industries – the legacy of the Revolution – or to run the buses. York was, in the '60s, largely white and English, and remains so today.

Based on the number of insurance cards held in York and the surrounding villages, York Employment Exchange in June 1965 numbered the workforce at 38,891 men and 25,500 women. In 1962, 26 per cent of working women worked in the chocolate industry (Rowntree and Terry), 18 per cent in professions and 16 per cent in distributive trades. For men it was 16 per cent in chocolate, 7.2 per cent (4,200 persons) in construction and 15 per cent in railways and transport. In total there were 8,500 workers at Rowntree in 1965 getting to work on thirteen special buses through the city to arrive at 7.30 a.m. and 1.30 p.m. and leaving at 12.30 p.m. and 4.30 p.m. Office staff arrived at 8.30 a.m. on three or four more buses leaving at 5.30 p.m. Sixty people from Selby came in on a special train to the Rowntree halt via York station. Night-shift workers had no transport laid on and no public transport; accordingly 50 per cent of them used bicycles.

We can break down the figures relating to employment in manufacturing even further. Between 1951 and 1971 those working specifically in cocoa and confectionery accounted for 50.2 per cent and 56.2 per cent of the workforce respectively: 9,570 and 9,520; railway carriage and wagon was 16.9 and 12.0 per cent (3,220 and 2,030); printing and publishing 6.7 per cent and 6.8 per cent (1,280 and 1,150); and glass and bricks, 3.3 per cent and 6.7 per cent (640 and 1,130). In the '60s, Rowntree allowed their workforce to

The aftermath of a rail accident when, on 28 October 1968, a DMU from York to Scarborough collided with a car on the crossing. The train driver, George Craven, was trapped in his cab for forty minutes. There were no other injuries, just lots of glass and shock.

reduce by some 25 per cent – it was mainly women's jobs that went; they were helped in this policy by increasing automation and a feeling locally in the town and in the firm that it was undesirable to have one company in such a dominant position. Moreover, there were difficulties hiring labour in York and the surrounding area.

More generally, 29 per cent worked in all forms of manufacturing at the end of the decade. The rest of employment demographic breaks down as follows: 8,080 in distribution; 2,290 or so in garages, hotels and restaurants; 3,340 in education; 3,060 in medical; 1,720 in finance; 224 in telephone, 1,560 in the post office, including ninety in the Lendal post office; 840 in gas, water and electricity; 250 professionals (dentists, bankers and the like); 510 in domestic service; 490 in defence (mainly the barracks); and forty-five Minster staff.

The first convent of the Sisters of the Second Order of Saint Francis was Plantation House in Hull Road in 1865; they moved to the obscure St Joseph's Monastery in Lawrence Street in 1873. Until recently they lived there behind twenty-feet-high walls, got up at 5.00 a.m., lived in silence, were vegetarians and cultivated a six-acre garden to make themselves largely self-sufficient. The convent comprised cloisters, cells, chapel and refectory. The remaining eight Poor Clare Colettines have now moved to Askham Bryan. The convent's Mother Abbess was obliged to seek permission from the Vatican for the move and admitted to mixed feelings: 'it's only bricks and mortar', she said.

Don't forget the nuns. The forty Poor Clare nuns came to York from Bruges.

British Rail employed about 1,700 office workers out of a within-the-walls total of 7,500. 700 children went to school here with 1,300 full time and 2,000 part-time students at the various colleges. Domestic service and manufacturing fell during the decade although education and medical, for example, rose. Military fell by 1,200 due to the amalgamation of two Yorkshire regiments. By and large, York's figures were in line with the rest of the country: the only exception was in transport and communications, in which York kept 14.4 per cent of the working population busy against a national figure of 6.6 per cent – accounted for by York becoming the HQ for Eastern Region of British Rail. Agriculture and mining (0.5 per cent and 4.3 per cent) were on the low side, as was manufacturing at 29 per cent compared with a national figure of 34 per cent.

The late sixties were exciting, turbulent times for Rowntree. First, in 1968, the huge American conglomerate, General Foods Corporation, put in an aggressive bid to buy the company. A stalwart defence was put up by the chairman, Donald Barron (now Sir), which was ultimately successful and the company remained independent. In 1969 Rowntree merged with Mackintosh and brought a strong portfolio containing such bestselling blockbusters as Rolo. In 1968 Rowntree's turnover was £78 million with a pre-tax profit of £4.3 million; in 1978 Rowntree Mackintosh Ltd was turning over £563 million with a pre-tax profit of £43 million.

York carriage works in the 60s. (Photo courtesy of York Press)

The new Post Office Sorting Office in Leeman Road. (Photo courtesy of York Press)

The Post Office Sorting Office in 1961 and 1968. (Photos courtesy of York Press)

In the '60s, in every year, over 3,700,000 or so passengers got on and off trains at the sixteen platforms of York station; 2,200 trains came and went, or 100 every hour. British Rail owned more land in York than the land area within the city walls.

In 1967 the Eastern and North Eastern regions of British rail amalgamated and relocated their headquarters from London to York. The new offices were built in the yard of the old, second York railway station (now council offices) next to the GNER headquarters, now a 5-star hotel. The railway carriage and wagon works was York's second biggest employer in the '60s. Wagon shop work was declining, though, and

York station in the '60s. (Photo courtesy of York Press)

closed in 1965 although this was offset by an increase in carriage maintenance work, leading to 600 extra jobs.

Cooke, Troughton & Simms and Vickers were the world's pre-eminent telescope manufacturers. In 1856, Cooke moved into the Buckingham Works, built on the site of the home of the second Duke of Buckingham at Bishophill – one of Britain's first purpose-built telescope factories. He built a telescope for Prince Albert in 1860 and one for a Gateshead millionaire; the telescope tube was thirty-two feet long and the whole instrument weighed nine tons – the biggest telescope in the world at the time. In 1893, H. D. Taylor, Optical Manager, designed the Cooke Photographic Lens, which has become the basic design for most camera lenses thereafter. In 1915 control of Cooke's was acquired by Vickers Ltd who had had an eye on Cooke's military products. Troughton & Simms was established in 1922; in 1939 the Haxby Road site was built. Of the 3,300 people employed by the firm, 1,400 were women. In the '60s the company traded as Vickers Instruments Ltd.

The first glassworks was opened in 1794 by Hampston & Prince near Fishergate making flint glass and medicinal phials. The York Flint Glass Company was set up in 1835 and by 1851 was a larger employer than either Terry or Craven. In 1930, it was incorporated as National Glass Works (York) Ltd, which became Redfearn National Glass Company in 1967; it was demolished in 1988 and replaced by the Novotel. Their speciality had been producing high quality glass bottles and jars for the soft drink trade, and white flint containers for food and pharmaceuticals.

Reconstruction and preservation work on St Martin's in Coney Street. (Photo courtesy of York Press)

F. W. Shepherd, the builders, developed the Portakabin in 1963 in a purpose-built factory in Huntington. In 1963 Terry's was bought by Forte for £4 million. In 1966 Craven, the sugar confectionery company moved out of Coppergate to a site in Poppleton. Anderton-Richardson, the fertilizer manufacturing company, was taken over by Hargreaves Fertilizers Ltd in 1967. Armstrong Patents Co were in Rawcliffe making suspension units for Ford cars with 2,000 workers in the late '60s.

Other names that would have been familiar in the 1960s include builders William Birch, founded in 1874, and whose projects have included work on York Minster Library, Fairfax House, King's Manor and the York Explore Library. And William Anelay, founded in 1874: they started in Doncaster, building many of the town's most prestigious properties including the impressive Mansion House there. In the early 1900s, the company relocated to York, due partly to the friendship between Thomas Anelay VI and architect Walter H. Brierley (the Yorkshire Lutyens) who encouraged the business to take advantage of the building and renovation opportunities available to it in York. At Leetham Flour Mill on Rowntree Wharf, part of which was taken over by Rowntree in 1937, tons of ingredients cocoa beans and gum arabic, were shipped from Hull docks right up to the landing stage there until 1967. Penty's Animal Feed Mill; Ben Johnson (founded in 1855) and Sessions, both printers were all active in the '60s. Sessions, in North Street and then from the 1920s, Huntington Road, was founded by Quaker William Alexander in 1811, as a bookshop and stationer's. Bellerby's saw mill thrived in Hungate. Another familiar sight would have been the cattle market, where the Barbican is now. In the '60s around 6,000 sheep and cattle were herded in and out of the forty-four stalls under the walls.

Craven's.

York cattle market in the 1960s. (Photo courtesy of York Press)

York's police force at the beginning of the '60s was around 179 men and eight women. A unified police force was formed in 1836. By 1855 the force was twenty-nine officers and men, and in addition, the first detective had been appointed. The force strength in 1885 was fifty-four and sixty-six in 1886. The first police station was the city commissioners' patrol, situated in St Andrewgate; it was taken over by the new force established in 1836 and not replaced until 1841 when a new station was built next to the fish market (now Silver Street). The station operating in the '60s (and still today) in Clifford Street was opened in 1892.

Napoleon arrived in York in 1822, one year after his death on St Helena. He stood sentinel first in Bridge Street for 153 years, outside Mrs Clarke's tobacconist, and then outside Judith Thorpe's tobacconist in Lendal, to whom letters were addressed simply as 'Napoleon, York' – and were delivered. Here in 1966 he is in full uniform, he is proffering a snuff box to David Handley of Whitby Street; Napoleon liked his snuff. He is carved out of a solid piece of oak and is the only known survivor of three made, each selling for £50.00. (Photo courtesy of York Press)

The sixties, then, was a typical decade for economics and employment in York. Just as during the Industrial Revolution, the city failed to attract new industry; what growth there was internal, with chocolate and railways remaining the dominant industries.

York was a minor Mecca for shopping in mid-Yorkshire. Only Leeds (twenty-four miles away to the south-west) and Harrogate (twenty-two miles to the east) got in the way. Beyond that you had to traipse to Hull (thirty-eight miles east), Scarborough (forty-one miles east) or even to Darlington (forty-nine miles north) for anything comparable. York of course, unlike Leeds in particular, had the added draw of manifold tourist attractions and specialist bijoux shops and good cafes.

Shopping in Parliament Street (1962) and Pavement (1965). (Photos courtesy of York Press)

Davygate in 1966. (Photos courtesy of York Press)

Familiar shops would have included Brown's department store in Davygate and Stubbs ironmonger's on Foss Bridge. Bookshops (remember them?) included Pickering's in Shambles and Godfrey's in Stonegate. There was Wright's the butchers and pie shop, Cox the cobbler in Shambles; Cussins & Light for cameras and electrical; Barnitt's for everything for the house in Colliergate, and Whitby Oliver for when you wanted to move that house.

This 'Mecca' had to satisfy some 106,000 York people in the estimated population for 1966, rising to 145,000 if Greater York – outskirts and outlying villages – is taken into consideration. Indeed, the shopping hinterland probably extended as far as Thirsk and Northallerton, Pickering and Malton, and Pocklington adding another 30,000 and making the market some 175,000 potential shoppers. In 1961 retail trade in the centre of York was estimated to be £14 million. The proportion of service to retail during the decade was steady at 13 per cent to 87 per cent.

York market in 1964, in Parliament Street; the fish market in Silver Street. (Photos courtesy of York Press)

The shopping experience in sixties York was rather varied. On Monday the city centre was very quiet with many shops closed; Wednesday afternoon was quieter still with half-day closing. The end of the week was progressively busier with Saturday afternoons hell on earth in the days when traffic was still permitted in all streets. Sundays, of course, were deserted. Eating out for lunch (or 'dinner' really) was part of that experience with a choice of Chinese and one Indian. Some shops had their restaurants and there was Terry's and self-service Bettys in St Helen's Square. The Yorkshire Club catered for the well-off on Lendal Bridge, and the City Club. Young's two clubs were very popular. Students hitched in from as far away as Hull for the pubs at the weekend or on Wednesdays, particularly Ye Olde Starre Inn in Stonegate.

The Shambles, Christmas 1969.

Chapter 6

A York Education

In the '60s over 700 children went to schools within the city, but many more criss-crossed on buses going to outlying schools. Over 600 full-time day and 2,000 evening-class students went back and forth from the Technical College. Exhibition Square was populated with 700 or so Art School students, along with some university students at King's Manor. Most students from the university lived in Acomb.

Archbishop Holgate's School is, after St Peter's, the oldest in York. It was founded as Archbishop Holgate's Grammar School in 1546 by Robert Holgate, Archbishop of York, financed by capital from the Dissolution of the Monasteries. The original grammar school was in Ogleforth and was known as the Reverend Shackley's School; one of the teachers was Thomas Cooke, the optical instrument manufacturer who went on to establish T. Cooke & Sons, later Cooke, Troughton & Simms, the famous telescope manufacturers. In 1858, the school merged with the Yeoman School when it moved to Lord Mayor's Walk; it relocated again in 1963 to its present site on Badger Hill.

Chemistry teacher Albert Holderness and John Lambert, both old boys of Archbishop Holgate's, were the authors of one of the most successful school chemistry books ever published: School Certificate Chemistry, published in 1936. The 500,000th copy came off the press in 1962 and the book remains in print today in its sixth edition, retitled A New Certificate Chemistry. Drama and music thrived at the school with many a barn dance and lots of jiving. 1961 saw a production of 'Let's Go Gay' while in 1962 the school reached the final of 'Top of the Form'. Archbishop Holgate was the only state school still to have boarders in the '60s.

York College for Girls was established in 1908 at No. 62 High Petergate in a fine building that is, in parts, at least 300 years old. After the school closed in 1997, it remained empty for eight years, then was refurbished and reopened as a restaurant, La Vecchia Scuola. The spirit of the old school is still very much alive: the owners have a permanent exhibition of many items of school memorabilia to evoke the atmosphere of the school, not least from the '60s. The first headmistress had the nickname E³, thanks to her initials – Elizabeth Emma Ellett. Miss Ellett and her two successors lived in the part of the school that is now Talbot Court; some of the girls boarded in the early days. In 1960, a new building was opened on what was the site of the old Fox Inn, and,

Half a million down and counting. (Courtesy of Archbishop Holgate School)

before that, in the seventeenth century, the Talbot Inn. This housed the chapel, library, science labs, home economics room and classrooms.

At the Minster School (the former Song School until 1986), the headmaster in 1962 still 'had a love of the old gym shoe as a disciplinary measure'; clubs included Song School, Loco-spotters, with visits to sheds at Leeds and Manchester on Wednesdays, stamp collecting, bird spotting and nature rambles. The year 1967 saw the end of free Wednesdays and of Saturday morning school. Art, craft and woodwork became compulsory for all boys. From the end of 1968 all boys had to stay to lunch; in 1969 the first school orchestra was formed and all pupils were obliged to learn an instrument. The old sloping desks were put on sale at 10s each, some dating back to 1903 with initials and dates carved into them. Until now, bicycle was the mode of transport for getting to the school; things were changing, though, as the (parents') cars started to take over. When they left at fourteen, most boys went on to Archbishop Holgate in the 1960s. In 1969 non-choristers outnumbered choristers (thirty-one to twenty-five) for the first time. The parents of pupils in the 1960s came from a wide variety of backgrounds, including, for fathers, brewery office manager, BR Motive Power supervisor, BR loco depot welder, company director, paint company rep, coach builder, potato merchant, market garden worker, wine and spirit merchant, decorator, watchmaker, journalist, engineer, electrician, mechanic, railway worker, teacher, headmaster and quantity surveyor. Mothers were mainly housewives and many were teachers, or else hotel cook, a secretary, professional actress and accounts clerk.

In 1969 the Bar Convent celebrated its bicentenary and marked the event with a renovation of the beautiful chapel, meticulously restoring its Georgian features.

The Victorian altar rail was discarded and a new altar made, using the side legs, cherubs and pelican – symbol of the Eucharist – giving its blood to feed its young from the original 1769 altar. The oak baroque figures representing the four Western Doctors of the Church were restored: Saints Jerome, Gregory, Augustine and Ambrose.

The Bar Convent of 1790 is the oldest lived-in convent in England, it was established as a school for Catholic girls in 1686 by Frances Bedingfield, an early member of Mary Ward's Institute, in response to Sir Thomas Gascoigne's demand: 'We must have a school for our daughters.' Sir Thomas, a local Catholic landowner, provided £450 to set up a boarding school; this was followed in 1699 by a free day school. Frances Bedingfield had been imprisoned in Ousebridge Gaol for her religious beliefs. The nuns, who still live here, belong to the Congregation of Jesus, which was founded by Mary Ward (1585–1645). For Catholics, the seventeenth century was often a time of persecution and the Bar Convent was very much a clandestine community. Known as 'the Ladies at the Bar', the sisters wore plain grey day dresses rather than habits to avoid raising suspicion. The community suffered great poverty, persecution and imprisonment – not just for their faith but also for teaching that faith. However, it survived, and in 1727 Elizabeth Stansfield and Ann Aspinal paid off the community's debts. In the 1760s, the original house was demolished and replaced with the fine Georgian house and integral chapel that can be visited today.

April 1769 saw the first Mass held in Mother Aspinal's beautiful new chapel, with its magnificent, but externally unobtrusive, neoclassical dome concealed beneath a pitched slate roof. Apart from the discreet dome, the building has many other integral features that betray the nature of its activities. The chapel is situated in the centre of the building so that it cannot be seen from the street, its plain windows reveal nothing of its ecclesiastical nature and there are no fewer than eight exits providing escape routes for the congregation in the event of a raid. There is also a priest hole still visible.

Later work to the Bar Convent in 1844 by G. T. Andrews resulted in an extension that included an enlarged day school and a conspicuous cross on the pediment. In the 1860s, the open courtyard at the centre of the building was glazed over. At this time the school was known locally as 'the poor school'. The floor is graced with tiles by Maws of Coalbrookdale. During the Great War, Belgian nuns and refugee children were accommodated in the convent and the concert hall was converted into a hospital ward for wounded soldiers. Tragedy struck in the Second World War during the 1942 Baedeker raids, when the convent was bombed and five sisters killed. The fifty pictures alongside the Bar Convent's 1987 staircase depict the life of Mary Ward. They were reproduced from seventeenth-century paintings in the Institute of Augsburg. The 2,000 or so books in the library date from between 1508 and 1850 and, unlike some library collections, they are well used and annotated. The convent also retains the preserved hand of St Margaret Clitherow. In 1977, the day school and boarding school eventually merged to become the Bar Convent Grammar School and boys were admitted for the first time; in 1985 it became part of All Saints' Roman Catholic School.

At the Minster there were in all twenty choristers and up to ten probationers and usually nine song men. After 1955 only the choristers sang weekday matins so that the song men might carry on other duties. There were three vicars-choral, the senior being sub chanter, another acting as chamberlain, and the third as headmaster of the Song School; they chanted the services, but no longer read the lessons.

The Wilberforce Memorial was the charity behind the Yorkshire School for the Blind; it was established at the King's Manor in response to the death of William Wilberforce in 1833 out of a desire to honour his memory and good works in as fitting a manner as possible. Wilberforce had represented Yorkshire as an MP for twenty-eight years and was an influential voice for the movement to abolish the slave trade and for the education and training of the blind. The school's mission was:

> To provide sound education together with instruction in manual training and technical work, for blind pupils, between the ages of five and twenty; to provide employment in suitable workshops or homes for a limited number of blind men and women who've lost their sight after the age of sixteen, in some occupation carried on at the school; and to promote such other agencies for the benefit of the blind as may enable them to gain their livelihood, or spend a happy old age.

Work done included weaving of Dales wool and acrylic materials into cardigans and sweaters, basket and mat making, microfilming, and mechanical, pneumatic and electrical sub-assembling. During the First World War the army ordered various products made by the pupils at the school. In 1963 the property housing the school at King's Manor was sold to the university and the school moved out to Dringhouses.

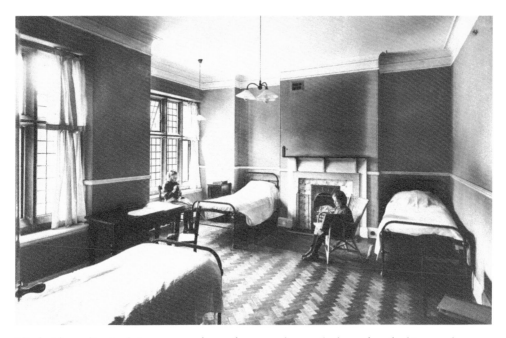

Blind girls reading in their rooms and a performance by pupils dressed as the kings and queens of England (*opposite*). (Courtesy of the Borthwick Institute)

School rules in the 1960s at the Quaker Mount School for (and still for) girls sound rather quaint by modern standards. On Sunday afternoons girls were allowed to go for walks with boys from Quaker Bootham school so long as there were at least two girls in the party; on Wednesday mornings fifth and sixth form girls were permitted to go into shops on the way back from the Clifford Street Quaker meeting – which they shared with Bootham boys – so long as they were not late back and any items bought were accounted for in their pocket money book; 'parole', or the freedom to go for walks on Saturday, Sunday or Wednesday afternoons, on condition that if and when they met friends or members of Bootham, they conducted themselves as if their parents or a member of staff were present. Breaking the rules led to being 'gated' – confined to school for one or more weeks. Cafés were strictly out of bounds unless accompanied by parents. Misbehaviour was often dealt with by a 'meditation', when the culprit was sent to her room to reflect on their poor conduct.

The consequences of the lowering of the age of maturity to eighteen was not lost on the headmistress at the Mount, Joyce Blake, in 1969 when some girls would be out of their parents' legal control on issues and policies relating to smoking, medical advice and treatment, drinking, sex and bedtime. In 1963 the school uniform was overhauled when the navy gymslip was replaced by a grey A-line skirt, grey V-neck jumper and a choice of red or blue striped blouses. Sixth formers still had to wear uniform but could forego the grey uniform overcoat. After school, trousers were allowed for the first time.

There were, of course, freedoms which attempted to keep the school and its pupils in tune with the times. Portable record players were allowed and an impromptu radio was set up so that girls could follow the aftermath of the assassination of John Kennedy.

After, this radio became a constant at breakfast time. A (successful) delegation was sent to the head to persuade her that watching Dr Who was the right thing to do for all sorts of reasons; permission was granted and the Dalek's electronic staccato echoed out of the school's one television. Helen Wainwright founded the Mount School branch of Amnesty International and later went on to edit *Red Pepper*; she was Ken Livingstone's Deputy Chief Economic Advisor to the Greater London Council and is a Fellow of the international think tank for progressive politics, the Transnational Institute, Amsterdam. In 1965 the swimming pool and gymnasium were opened.

The story of the Mount School begins with Esther Tuke, second wife of William Tuke, who in 1785 opened the boarding school in Trinity Lane, off Micklegate and known then as the Friends' Girls School. The aims of the York school were heavily influenced by the famous Quaker school at Ackworth near Pontefract, which was founded in 1779 by John Fothergill and which, in turn, was previously a (particularly insalubrious) branch of the London Foundling Hospital in Bloomsbury. Fothergill, a Quaker physician, teamed up with William Tuke and David Barclay (of banking fame) to open the school for Quaker children 'not of affluence'. Despite their best intentions, it had a reputation for being harsh, if not barbarous".' By 1796, Trinity Lane could not accommodate the thirty or so girls and so purpose-built premises were bought for £450 in Tower Street near to York Castle and the Friends' Meeting House.

Mount girls in a Granada Television episode of Top of the Form in the 1960s. (Courtesy of the Mount School)

William Tuke eventually retired in 1804, but the school was in financial difficulties and closed in 1812. In 1829, Samuel Tuke established the York Friends' Boys' School (later Bootham School) and then turned his attentions to establishing a girls' equivalent along the same lines. The York Quarterly Meeting Girls School materialised in Castlegate House in 1831, the 1763 mansion of the Recorder of York. The day was long at Castlegate, with lessons from 7.00 a.m. to 5.00 p.m. followed by private study for an hour at 7.00 p.m. and scripture readings from 8.00 p.m. Lessons included Latin, Greek, arithmetic, mathematics, art, grammar, French and posture. Posture was not popular, involving as it did instruction on how to bow, shake hands and stand with pointed toes.

The Mount girls attended lectures given by the Yorkshire Philosophical Society, adding to and annotating their own collections of shells, minerals and pressed plants. In 1855, the lease on Castlegate expired, thus triggering the move to the purpose-built buildings at the Mount: 353 girls had been educated and fifty-four had completed teacher training at Castlegate. The Mount School opened its doors in 1857 under the supervision of Rachel Tregelles. The girls lived four or five to a bedroom rather than in dormitories and enjoyed the luxury of internal flushing toilets and hot water on tap. Fees were £47 11s 2d per year. Lydia Rous took over as superintendent of the Mount School in 1866 and it was she who ensured that Mount girls entered the new public examinations. The University of London was not interested; to it, 'girls were poorly educated and therefore incapable of taking a degree course' but the University of Cambridge, which established Emily Davies' Girton College for women in 1873, took them on board. From about 1912, a shift in admissions policy took place, allowing more and more non-Quaker children into the Mount School, which hitherto had been almost exclusively Quaker. By the 1930s, half of the 130 pupils were from outside the Society of Friends. In the Second World War Mount School girls joined the Land Girls and became nurses. The school took in three refugees saved by the Kindertransport movement. Alumni of the main school include actors Mary Ure and Dame Judi Dench, the three Drabble sisters (A. S. Byatt, Margaret Drabble and Helen Langdon), astronomer Jocelyn Bell Burnell, Helen Wainwright, and TV correspondent Kathy Killick.

In the '60s York had fifteen mixed secondary modern schools, nine of which no longer exist including Margaret Clitherow, Acomb, St Wilfred's and Derwent. Huntington School opened in 1966. Knavesmire Secondary Modern moved to Middlethorpe in 1964 admitting boys for the first time in 1965, later becoming the College of Law. Manor School was bombed in the 1942 Baedeker raid, merging with Priory Street school and converting from boys only to mixed; it moved to Low Poppleton Lane in 1965.

Northfield School opened in 1965 as Northfield Open-Air School for children with chronic physical disabilities. Fulford County Secondary School started in 1964 while Fulford Cross Special School opened its doors in 1965 on the site of Fulford Open-Air School. This originally was at No. 11 Castlegate in 1913 in the same building as the Tuberculosis Dispensary; it moved in 1914 to a converted army hut in the grounds of Fulford House and became known as Fulford Road School for Delicate and Partially Sighted Children. The open-air school movement was set up in 1904 in Berlin to curb the development of tuberculosis in children and, as such, required the establishment of schools that combine medical care with teaching adapted to pupils with pre-tuberculosis. Fulford closed in 1960 and was demolished in 1964. The pupils were transferred to Northfield School.

St Margaret's Church of England school opened in Castlegate in 1905, moving to 54 Micklegate with 188 girls (aged 5–17) and ten lucky boys, closing there in 1968. St Margaret Clitherow Girls Secondary Modern was originally Blessed Margaret Clitherow School for Girls opened in 1963 in Bad Bargain Lane absorbing St Wilfred's senior pupils, which then remained a primary school.

The York and Ripon Diocesan Training College for schoolmasters, later known as St. John's (now York St John University), was opened in May 1841 as a residential training school for the diocese of York. Teaching and residential accommodation was increased by annexes in Gray's Court in 1946, Heworth Croft in 1950 and The Limes in 1953. A biology laboratory was built in 1950, a library in 1952, a lecture theatre in 1954, and an arts and crafts block in 1955. There were around 267 students in the sixties. The York Model School (used for teaching practice), or St John's Voluntary Aided Secondary Modern School for boys (200 of them in 1956), closed in 1965. It had opened in 1859 as a demonstration school with 338 boy boarders in 1899. Fees were 7s 6d per quarter: Latin, shorthand and French were extra.

York School of Art thrived in the '60s when it was based in Exhibition Square. Before that it had a circuitous journey: in 1842 it was established in Little Blake Street as York School of Design, as a branch of the Normal School of Design in London; in 1848 it relocated to Minster Yard as York School of Art, in the premises vacated by St Peter's School moving to Exhibition Square in 1892. Two studios were acquired in Marygate

Field Marshal Vicount Montgomery inspecting the cadets at St Peter's School in 1962. (Courtesy of St Peter's Archive)

Building bridges over Bootham at St Peter's. (Courtesy of St Peter's Archive)

in 1949 when there were 594 students, of whom thirty-two attended full-time. Since 2007, it has been York College of Fine Art, Craft and Design at York College.

The University of York was finally established in 1963 in Heslington Hall and King's Manor in York city centre. It is officially described as 'a research-intensive plate glass university'. This collegiate university has now expanded to include a medical school, which it operates with the University of Hull. Medical education in Hull and York goes back to the three following institutions: Hull Medical School (1831), York Medical Society (1832) and the York Medical School (1834). In 2003 the University of York attracted the highest research income per capita of any UK university. It is among the top twenty universities in Europe, and the top ninety universities in the world, according to the 2010 QS World University Rankings. It was named the *Sunday Times* University of the Year in 2003 and *Times* Higher Education University of the Year in 2010 for its 'success in combining academic excellence with social inclusion, as well as its record in scientific discovery'. The *Times University Guide* said of York that 'the university is increasingly recognised as a permanent fixture in the top rank of British higher education' and that 'no university had a better record for teaching quality'. The *Sunday Times* said, 'York is one of Britain's academic success stories, forging a reputation to rival Oxford and Cambridge in the space of forty years. In teaching it has a recent track record better than Oxford, according to the official assessments of teaching quality.'

York's predilection for social sciences and science did its case no harm at all. Indeed, its position in the middle of three great urban industrial areas – Teesside, Humberside and the West Riding – made a university at York very apposite. Furthermore, the fact that Seebohm Rowntree had lived in York and based much of his social scientific research on the city and its people, added further credibility to the application. The existence of the Borthwick Institute of Historical Research (then in St Antony's Hall) and the Institute of Advanced Architectural Studies (in the secularised St John's church in Micklegate) only strengthened York's credentials.

In 1963 there were 216 undergraduates, fourteen postgraduates, and twenty-eight academic and administrative staff looking after six departments: Economics, Education, English, History, Mathematics and Politics. The linguistics department was one of the first in the UK. In December 2014 there were 15,353 students. In 1964, work began on purpose-built structures on the Heslington Campus.

Baron James of Rusholme, the university's first Vice-Chancellor, said initially that the university 'must be collegiate in character, that it must deliberately seek to limit the number of subjects and that much of the teaching must be done via tutorials and seminars'. Graeme Moodie, founding head of the Politics Department, insisted that students be involved in the governance of the university at all levels, a model which has since been widely adopted elsewhere. Vice-Chancellor Eric James echoed the textbook success of his colleagues at Archbishop Holgate School just down the road: he was co-author of the best-selling *James and Hall's Elementary Chemistry*; he went on to teach at Manchester Grammar School and was a member of the Brains Trust.

York's first two Colleges, Derwent and Langwith, were founded in 1965, and were followed by Alcuin and Vanbrugh in 1967 and Goodricke in 1968. In 1972 Wentworth College opened. Study bedrooms were functional and practical, furnished

Life at the new university: student room in college, the library and the dinner ladies, all at Heslington. (Photos courtesy of York University)

with plain, heavily textured fabric and hessian and light wood furniture reflecting the serious but modern atmosphere.

To paraphrase the University website, in October 1963 a welcome reception was organised by the Friends of York Art Gallery – hosted by Sir Herbert Read – with many of the city's great and the good present. Later that month, a service to commemorate the inauguration of the University was held in York Minster. The King's Manor was the social centre, with staff and students socialising in the Cellar Club which, with its rough brick walls, low vaulted ceilings and coloured lights built into the floor. The blues singer T-bone Walker was among those who played there. The community was young, keen and liberal-minded. Some of the young academics returned from teaching posts in the States to work at York; the average age of the professors was a youthful forty. During the first year all students lived in digs, bussing out to the university where Heslington Hall, the Stables and the New Building housed all the lectures, study and catering facilities. In 1964 English, Education, History and Philosophy were moved out, or in, to the King's Manor.

During the decade the university was developed and built on schedule and five colleges, three laboratory-based buildings, Central Hall, the Library, the Sports Hall, Music Centre and the Jack Lyons Concert Hall were all completed. The 1960s ended with 2,500 undergraduate students, twelve times the original intake. The covered walkways were innovations in the 1960s while the 'CLASP' buildings and the lake were criticised as extravagant features, although the lake was an essential part of the construction to allow building on such marshy land. The ducks and geese (nice but somewhat messy) were bought from Sir Peter Scott's Wildlife Centre; it is the largest

The King's Manor as university departments. (Courtesy of York Press)

plastic-bottomed lake in Europe. The campus also supports a large rabbit population, the hunting of which by students is strictly prohibited.

Conferences were always going to be important in the university's business plan, so much so that revenues derived from conferences soon exceeded that from tuition fees.

The first petition for a university in York was to King James I in 1617. In 1903, F. J. Munby and others (including the Yorkshire Philosophical Society) proposed a 'Victoria University of Yorkshire'. What was then the College of Ripon and York St John considered purchasing Heslington Hall as part of a proposed new campus. Heslington Hall is a fine Elizabethan manor built by Thomas Eymes in 1568; Eymes was secretary to Henry VIII's Great Council of the North, which had its headquarters in King's Manor. As with other buildings of the time, it was constructed in the shape of an 'E' in honour of Elizabeth I.

The first Chancellor was George Lascelles, 7th Earl of Harewood (1962–1967) and he was followed by Kenneth Clark, Lord Clark (1967–1978), of BBC TV series *Civilisation* fame. Harriet Harman a Labour MP for Camberwell & Preston since 1997 studied for a BA (Hons) in Politics at the university in the late 1960s.

The York Student Television station was founded at the university in 1967 and is England's oldest student television station. YSTV once held the world record for longest continuous television broadcast under a single director. *Nouse*, from the ancient Greek *nous*, meaning intellect, or common sense, with a nod also to the River Ouse, was the first student newspaper and website at the University of York. It is the oldest registered society of, and funded by, the University of York Students' Union. *Nouse* was founded in 1964 by student Nigel Fountain.

The prestigious and world famous Borthwick Institute is now housed at the university; when it first opened it immediately attracted both academic researchers and genealogists, and during the first twenty years search room users increased from 405 in 1956 to 1,276 in the academic year 1968–9 and 1,748 in the year 1970–1.

In the early days, the Borthwick Institute occupied only the medieval hall wing of St Anthony's Hall, with search rooms, strong rooms, a teaching room and offices while the rest of the complex was used for the City of York's Day Continuation School for young people studying on day release from work. The School moved out in 1969 and the Borthwick – by then badly needing facilities and space – took over some of the vacated buildings: the east wing was converted into a ground floor library with large conservation room above, and a staff room was created in part of the north block. The west wing was then leased by the University to York Archaeological Trust who occupied it for more than twenty years. The Borthwick expanded into the whole of the St Anthony's Hall buildings in 1995.

Bibliography

Borthwick Institute for Archives: www.york.ac.uk/borthwick
Fairfax House: http://www.fairfaxhouse.co.uk/
York Archaeological Trust: www.yorkarchaeology.co.uk
York Art Gallery: http://www.yorkartgallery.org.uk/
Yorkshire Archaeological Society: http://www.yas.org.uk/
Yorkshire Architectural and York Archaeological Society: http://www.yayas.org/
York City Archives: www.york.gov.uk/info/200424/archives/351/archives
York Civic Trust: http://www.yorkcivictrust.co.uk
York Evening Decorative & Fine Art Society: www.nadfas.org.uk
York Family History Society: www.yorkfamilyhistory.org.uk
York Georgian Society: http://www.yorkgeorgiansociety.org
York Railway Museum oral history of railway men and women: www.nrm.org.uk/
NRM/RailwayStories/railwayvoices.aspx

Acknowledgements

As with *York in the 1950s* many of the images in the book are from the superb archive of photographs held by *The Press* in York. Thanks then go out again to Anne Green, Steve Lewis and Perry Austin-Clarke for their generosity and the work they have done sourcing and reproducing the pictures for me. As usual, the pictures are theirs but the captions are all mine – so any errors of fact are entirely my fault. You can see, or add to, the *Press* archive at www.press.co.uk/memories.

John Hattam was kind enough to give permission to use the Clifton Green Primary School picture. Thanks also to Jenny Orwin at Bootham School; Susannah Harrison at the University of York; Jacqui Sissons, Archbishop Holgate School; Pat Chandler, St Peter's School ; Sarah Sheils, The Mount School; Rachel Wade, at York Museums Trust for the James Lloyd Clifford's Tower artwork which hangs in the newly refurbished City of York Art Gallery; Ian Drake at YAYAS; Alexandra Medcalf and Dr Amanda Jones at the Borthwick Institute for Archives; Colin Bradley, formerly of the Road Runners, for the group picture, including Paul Rodgers of Free, and the Ford Consul.

Front cover illustration: a scene from the Kavern Club in York's Micklegate in 1964. (*Photo Courtesy of York Press*)
Back cover illustration: the ducks and geese on the campus at York University soon after its opening in 1963. (Photo courtesy of York Press)

BELFAST ON A PLATE

BELFAST
ON A PLATE

PHOTOGRAPHY BY
DAVID PAULEY – THE STUDIO
WRITTEN BY
JOANNA BRANIFF

CONTENTS

FOREWORD

I heard Rory McIlroy talking on TV today. He said: 'In sport Northern Ireland always punches above its weight!' Hey fella ... not just in sport! I reckon that Belfast is in the top three provincial food cities in the UK and it's been up there for quite some time. I'm always proud to entertain visitors and to dazzle them by showing off our fine restaurants and hospitality.

For visitors it's the hospitality that they notice first. They can't believe how warm and genuine that good ole 'Norn Iron' welcome really is. How folks seem to make time for a wee chat and a bit of craic. Hey, it's in our nature! We want you to think well of us and to find out where you're from, are you having a good time and did ya get a good feed!

Good restaurants are in the hospitality business, maybe even more so than the food business. It's the price of entry if you want to be one of the 'top boys'. This is what binds all the fabulous restaurants in 'Belfast On A Plate'.

I believe that great restaurants must have a vision of who and what they want to be and not copycats of someone else's concept. You can be inspired of course by your favourite restaurants around the globe but it's the personalities and each individual vision or mission that sets them apart, be they chefs, managers or owners. We seem particularly good at this in Belfast. It's a small city and many of us have left home to train or travel abroad, then brought back here those experiences to the benefit of Belfast.

Couple that with a sense of love, pride, hard work, fantastic produce and you have a pretty damn good recipe for great restaurants.

Our produce of course is our crowning glory. The farmers, fishermen, producers, butchers etc are never far away because we're such a small province. It's not unusual for a butcher to know exactly the fields that the beef and lamb are grazing on and many of our fishermen are 'day boats' so they sell what they catch that day. This small-scale hands-on approach gives us world-class meat, fish, game, cheese, butter etc ... truly world class!

What's great to see nowadays is the spread of different styles of restaurants for different occasions. We've got the uber cool urban cafés / restaurants, the neighbourhood owner-operated bistros and the chic special occasion Michelin-starred experience. One thing that pleases me is that there is a maturity to the cooking in Belfast. The cooking nowadays is proper good cooking with skill, experience, well judged flavours and concepts. I have my favourite restaurants and chefs but I think it's safe to say that this is just personal taste. Looking at the list of restaurants in 'Belfast On A Plate', wow they're all great ... Belfast really has come of age! Keep 'er lit fellas!

Paul Rankin

INTRODUCTION

They say you can tell a lot about a city by its food culture. If that's true, Belfast has a lot to be proud of. The city now boasts a plethora of world-class eateries, two Michelin-starred restaurants, chilled out bistros and exceptional gastro pubs. The talented and committed chefs and restaurateurs behind this gastronomic revolution are substantial contributors to the exciting vibe currently invigorating Belfast's tourist economy and attracting local people to enjoy the food of their city.

2016 marks Northern Ireland's Year of Food and Drink, celebrating and showcasing the best local produce and promoting the people whose lives are dedicated to rearing, making, cooking and serving it. It is fitting that the hard work of these food heroes is being recognised as they have worked tirelessly together for decades to create an impressive supply network delivering consistent excellence. A close symbiotic relationship has developed between local growers, artisan producers and the chefs they supply, bringing together the people in our community who care most passionately about food. This means fresh, locally grown produce is featuring prominently on modern menus. The exceptional quality of Northern Irish produce is undeniable. Fish and seafood from our pristine seas and loughs are being enjoyed at home, as well as being exported all over the world. Beef from our grass-fed cattle remains a favourite on local menus but is also prized in France and Germany.

Many of our artisan producers have collected international awards and plaudits for their specialty cheeses, oils and dressings, preserves and dairy products. This natural homegrown bounty is being employed by our talented and visionary chefs to build Belfast's global reputation for food excellence.

In the last 15 years, Belfast has blossomed into a flourishing, modern city and is now recognised as one of the great European food destinations. This book tells the individual stories of the chefs and restaurant owners who have helped put Belfast firmly on the gastronomic map. The city's impressive contemporary restaurant scene has been developing and flourishing since 1989 and has been built on the work of three waves of dynamic and innovative chefs. In the early 1990s, the first wave of pioneering chefs, Nick Price, Michael Deane and Paul Rankin kickstarted a food revolution when they bravely opened their groundbreaking Belfast eateries at a time when trading conditions in the city were less than ideal. Nick's Warehouse, Deanes and Roscoff restaurants changed not just how the people of Belfast eat but also our entire food culture by engendering a sense of pride and confidence in locally produced food. They scooped a galaxy of Michelin stars and attracted positive international attention to the city, setting the highest standards in terms of quality and range in fine and casual dining.

They also provided the inspiration and training for a second wave of ambitious and talented chefs including Niall McKenna (James St. South and Hadskis), Tony O'Neill (Coppi and Il Pirata), Simon McCance (The Ginger Bistro), Andy Rea (Mourne Seafood Bar), Cath Gradwell (Neill's Hill), Brian McCann (Shu), Alan Foster (Tedfords and Tedfords Kitchen), Michael O'Connor (The Barking Dog), John Paul Leake (The Merchant Hotel) and Marty Murphy (Howard Street). Most of these second wave chefs got their initial taste of professional kitchen training under the first wave innovators. Inspired by their exceptional mentors, many then embarked on food odysseys of their own around the world. Returning home, they have brought back the exciting flavours and techniques learned in other cultures and marinated them with our own traditional dishes and local produce to create a unique and impressive Belfast food signature.

There is total confidence in the future development of the city's food culture as a third wave of young, dedicated chefs has firmly picked up the torch of the pioneers. They are well trained, well travelled and bursting with enthusiasm and optimism. Hungry for success, they are opening their own award-winning restaurants, heading up demanding kitchens, winning Michelin stars while pushing the boundaries of exciting international cuisine utilising and promoting the best local ingredients.

Chefs Chris Fearon (Deanes at Queens), Danielle Barry (Deanes Eipic), Tim Fetherston (General Merchants), John Moffatt (Graze), Cathal Duncan (Hadskis), David Gillmore (James St. South), Patrick Rowan (Saphyre), Gareth McCaughey (The Muddlers Club) and Stephen Toman (OX) are fuelling an appetite in Belfast for innovative food built on the freshest indigenous produce.

All of these chefs and restaurateurs share a deep pride in Belfast and the resilience of its people. Quietly working behind the scenes in their kitchens, these unsung heroes provide the vital memorable food experiences for the city's throngs of tourists, make the special occasion memories for locals and create thousands of jobs, while contributing massively to the economy and energy of Belfast. In this book, they share not only their own personal stories but also 60 of their signature recipes so you can enjoy a taste of Belfast at home. Belfast On A Plate is a distillation of the city's contemporary food scene, featuring stories and recipes from some of our most talented chefs. Their personal culinary philosophies, diverse backgrounds, wide range of influences and engaging life stories simmer together to create the unique flavour of Belfast. We invite you to enjoy a taste!

Joanna Braniff

COPPI

TONY O'NEILL

COPPI: TONY O'NEILL

Tony O'Neill is one of the second wave of influential chefs in the Belfast restaurant scene having had major roles establishing some of the city's finest eateries. His list of credits includes the Waterfront Hall, The Merchant Hotel and Beatrice Kennedy's, where he served as Executive Chef at their inceptions. He is now running some of Belfast's most popular restaurants, overseeing and inspiring the menus of Coppi and Il Pirata, along with the newest property in the group, Bartali in Portballintrae, while enthusiastically nurturing young, up-and-coming chefs.

Tony is a man of quiet passion, easy charm and openness and his food ethos reflects his personality. Born in Australia in 1972 of parents who emigrated from Northern Ireland, Tony came back with his family to the city he regards as home in 1982. His childhood years in Australia exposed him to a multicultural society that was a melting pot for international cuisine and fusion food. These early life experiences infused him with a gastronomic wanderlust reflected in his menus today. It also gave him a relaxed 'can do' spirit and warmth towards people – meaning everyone is welcome at his table.

He returned to Australia aged 21 and worked his way through some of the country's best restaurant kitchens, learning and being influenced by what he describes as a 'magpie' approach to food. It formed the basis of '90s Antipodean fusion cuisine: choose the best flavours, cooking methods and ingredients from different food cultures, rip up the rulebook and reassemble them to create a new fresh style.

He even spent a year of his youth travelling the expanse of Australia living in a campervan and working in a variety of kitchens so he could have a food journey encompassing as many different tastes and preparation methods as possible. All of which can still be subtly tasted in his food today, although now he has returned to the more simple, traditional and rustic Italian home-cooking style. His personal favourite food is lasagne. For him it conjures up memories of family, warmth, love and sharing over the dinner table.

Tony O'Neill lacks any sense of pretension regarding the food he serves. He is a self-confessed 'big picture' chef with an innate understanding of the whole dining experience but with a passion for quality in the detail. His food is simple and uncomplicated, made with the very best fresh local ingredients. His determination to ensure his core ingredients are perfect is reflected in his approach to homemade pasta. Trial, error, perseverance and huge customer demand has lead to him setting up his own pasta factory in East Belfast, which now services his restaurants with a daily supply of delicious fresh pasta – the hero of many of his dishes.

He has an air of understated confidence and a wealth of accumulated knowledge gained through experience and observation. Central to his cooking ethos is an understanding of what makes people truly happy. He believes in relaxed informality, companionship and bonding over shared food experiences. While daily specials provide inspired seasonal highlights, he doesn't mess with his core menu, as he knows his customers well enough to realise they keep coming back for more of the same because it's just so good. His inspired Cichetti (or small snack plates) include dishes of Beef Brisket and Gorgonzola Polpettine or Duck Ravioli Fritti with Truffle Porcini Mayo that demand to be shared, while his Duck Ragù and Smoked Chicken Tortellini dishes remain menu stalwarts that customers repeatedly revisit like old friends.

Tony's other great passion in life is cycling. That's why the three restaurants in the group are all named after his Italian cycling heroes, Il Pirata (Marco Pantani's nickname), Coppi after Fausto Coppi and Bartali after Gino Bartali. And there are comparisons to be drawn between racing cyclist Fausto Coppi – Il Campionissimo or champion of champions and Tony himself.

To be this confident and competent as a chef, it takes endurance, vision and stamina built on a foundation of passion and energy. Combine those qualities with decades of experience and a 360-degree understanding of the restaurant industry and you will begin to appreciate the enormous contribution Tony O'Neill has made to the success of the modern Belfast restaurant scene.

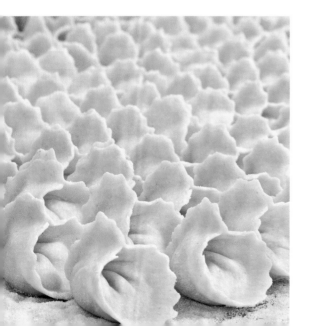

PORK SCALOPPINI

Serves 4

Gnocchi

500g very dry mashed
    potato, still warm
1 large egg
75g fine semolina
50g plain flour
50g Parmesan, grated
50g butter
Maldon salt and black
    pepper to taste
50g parsley, chopped

Pork and Sauce

1 tbsp olive oil for cooking
plain flour seasoned with salt
    and ground black pepper
600g pork loin, fat removed
    and thinly sliced
50g butter
200g chestnut mushrooms,
    thinly sliced
2 medium shallots, finely diced
2 cloves garlic, roughly chopped
150ml Marsala wine
100ml single cream
200g spinach, washed and dried
salt and freshly ground black
    pepper to season

Garnish

fresh rocket
balsamic vinegar
olive oil
Maldon salt
shaved Parmesan

Method

1. For the Gnocchi, place the mash into a large bowl and season well. Add the eggs and mix until all the egg has been absorbed by the potato. Add the two types of flour and grated Parmesan mix to incorporate; do not over mix as the potato will continue to absorb the flours, making them very heavy and dense. 2. Lightly flour a work surface and place the gnocchi mix on top, knead very lightly until the dough feels barely sticky and has come together. 3. Place a large pot of water onto high heat and bring to the boil. Pull sections of the dough and roll into a long sausage shape, cut to desired size and place on a floured tray. Have a large tub of iced water ready. 4. Drop the gnocchi into the boiling water and cook for a couple of minutes. When the gnocchi is ready it will rise to the surface of the pot. Remove from the water and plunge into iced water. Allow to cool completely then drain thoroughly. 5. Toss the cooked gnocchi in olive oil and store in the fridge. 6. To cook the gnocchi, place a large pan over medium heat and add a little butter. When the butter starts to foam add the cooled potato gnocchi, cook in the butter until golden brown all over. Remember the gnocchi is already cooked so you are just heating it through and crisping the outside. Season to taste with Maldon salt and black pepper and sprinkle over the parsley. Place into a warm bowl ready to be served.

7. For the Pork and Sauce, heat a wide non-stick frying pan over a medium heat, add one tablespoon of olive oil. Place the seasoned flour onto a flat tray and coat the slices of pork with the flour. Dust off any excess flour and set aside until the oil has heated. 8. Add the pork to the pan and cook over medium heat for 2–3 minutes or until it begins to colour and turn golden, turn the pork and immediately drain off the oil before adding the butter, mushrooms, shallots and garlic. Allow to cook until the butter begins to foam and the mushrooms have softened. 9. Add the Marsala wine and bring to the boil. Continue to boil until the wine has reduced by three quarters. Remove the pork from the sauce at this stage and place on a warm plate. 10. Add the single cream and allow to come to the boil. Add the spinach and allow the sauce to reduce until it coats the back of a spoon. 11. Season to taste, return the pork to the pan and immediately remove from the heat.

Assembly

Spoon the pork flat on to a plate. Place the rocket into a bowl. Mix together the balsamic vinegar and olive oil. Season with Maldon salt and add the shaved Parmesan. Mix together well and serve on the side along with the potato gnocchi.

Coppi

PORTAVOGIE PRAWN TORTELLINI, BUTTER POACHED LOBSTER TAIL AND TARRAGON

Serves 4

Prawn Tortellini

500g fresh Portavogie prawn tails
2 cloves garlic
juice and zest ½ lemon
20g melted butter
20ml double cream
25g breadcrumbs, finely blended
1 egg, beaten
1 tbsp tarragon, finely chopped
salt and pepper to taste
500g fresh egg pasta

Lobster and Butter

50g butter
1 clove garlic, crushed
juice and zest ½ lemon
75ml fish stock
25ml dry vermouth
1 small lobster tail shell
    removed, reserve the claws
    for another use
1 tbsp chopped tarragon
2 plum tomatoes blanched,
    seeded, peeled and diced
salt and pepper to season

Garnish

samphire
asparagus, thinly shaved
fresh basil and tarragon

Method

1. For the Prawn Tortellini, place the prawns, garlic, lemon juice and zest into a blender and blend until smooth. With the machine still running slowly, add the melted butter and cream until everything has incorporated. Remove from blender and add breadcrumbs and egg. Mix well. Add the chopped tarragon, salt and pepper. If the mix is wet, add more breadcrumbs then chill in the refrigerator for 2 hours. **2.** To fill the tortellini, place sheet of pasta on a lightly floured surface with the long side parallel to the edge of work surface. Place eight heaped teaspoons of the prawn filling along the top third of the sheet about 10cm apart. Using a 7cm pastry cutter, cut around the mixture. Moisten pasta around each mound of filling using a pastry brush dipped in water. Fold the dough up and over the filling to enclose and make semi-circle shapes; press around filling to seal and remove any excess air. Transfer to prepared baking sheet. Cover with a clean kitchen towel. Repeat with remaining dough and filling. Now pick up each individual semi-circle and pinch the two ends together. Chill until ready to cook. **3.** To cook the tortellini, bring a large pot of salted water to the boil. Add about 6–8 per serving and cook until tender but al dente (about 2 minutes).

4. For the Lobster and Butter, in a small pot gently heat the butter with the garlic, lemon juice and zest, fish stock and vermouth until it emulsifies. Gently place the lobster tail in and immerse under the liquid, reduce the heat to a light simmer and allow to poach for 6–8 minutes until just cooked. **5.** Remove the pot from the heat and immediately add the tarragon and diced tomato. Adjust seasoning and keep warm until ready to serve.

Assembly

Heat a heavy-based pot of water to a rolling boil, remove the lobster from the butter and slice into thin medallions. Heat the sauce gently without boiling rapidly, in the meantime drop the pasta in the water to boil for approximately 2–3 minutes until floating and al dente to touch. Remove the pasta from the water and drain, place the lobster meat in a pasta bowl, spoon over a little sauce and finally assemble the tortellini in the bowl. Finish the dish by spooning over a little more sauce, garnish with cooked samphire, shaved asparagus and the freshly torn basil and tarragon. Serve at once.

Coppi

DUCK RAGÙ, PORCINI MUSHROOM RAVIOLI, TRUFFLE AND PARMESAN

Serves 4

Duck Legs
4 female duck legs
200g Maldon salt
2 cloves garlic, left whole
3 sprigs thyme
1 litre duck or goose fat

Mushroom Ravioli
50g butter
1 shallot, finely diced
1 clove garlic, crushed
300g button mushrooms, sliced
200g dried porcini mushrooms,
    soaked in cold water
    until softened
50ml truffle oil
20g parsley, chopped
Maldon salt and fresh
    black pepper to taste
500g fresh egg pasta

Duck Stock
1kg duck carcass, skin
    and fat removed
2 sticks celery
1 large onion
2 medium carrots
2 bay leaves
6 sprigs thyme
200ml red wine
2½ litres water

Duck Ragù
2 shallots, finely diced
3 garlic cloves
1 stick celery, diced
250ml red wine
1 tbsp fresh thyme leaves

To Serve
truffle oil
shaved Parmesan
chopped parsley

Method

1. For the Duck Legs, preheat oven to 140°C. Pat legs dry and salt well. Rest at room temperature for at least 20 minutes and in fridge overnight. **2.** Put in a small casserole dish, skin side up. Add garlic and thyme and pour over the duck fat, wrap with tin foil and cook until very tender (1½–2 hours). Remove from oven and cool, then remove from the fat and peel off all skin. Crisp skin in oven at 140°C to garnish the finished dish. **3.** Remove meat from the legs and place in a bowl. Spoon two tablespoons of duck fat into the bowl and season. Reserve for ragù. **4.** For the Mushroom Ravioli, place butter in a large pan, add shallots and garlic. Cook over low heat for 5 minutes or until soft with no colour. Turn up heat and add mushrooms, cook until all moisture has evaporated. Add soaked porcini mushrooms and a little of its soaking liquid. Cook until all liquid has evaporated. Remove from heat and stir in truffle oil, chopped parsley and season with salt and pepper. Allow to cool overnight. **5.** To fill the ravioli, place sheet of pasta on a lightly floured surface. Place eight heaped teaspoons of mushroom filling along top third of sheet, 10cm apart. Moisten pasta around each mound of filling with pastry brush dipped in water. Fold dough up and over filling to enclose; press around filling to seal. Cut between mounds with a plain pastry wheel, use fluted pastry wheel to cut into square ravioli. Transfer to prepared baking sheet and cover. Chill until ready to cook.

6. To cook the ravioli, bring a large pot of salted water to the boil. Add about 6–8 ravioli per serving and cook until tender but al dente (about 2 minutes). **7.** For the Duck Stock, place duck bones on large roasting tray and roast until golden, 220°C. Remove and drain well. Place in pot, cover with cold water and bring to the boil. Toss vegetables in a little duck fat and roast, drain well and add to the stock. **8.** Pour off excess fat from roasting tray and deglaze pan with red wine. When boiling, add to stock. Skim any scum and turn down to simmer. Add bay leaves and thyme, simmer for 2 hours, skimming all the time. Strain stock, discard bones and vegetables. **9.** Place strained stock in a large pan and bring to the boil, reduce to a simmer until the stock has reduced by half. Remove from heat and reserve. **10.** For the Duck Ragù, place wide pan over low heat. Add a little duck fat and sweat onion, garlic and celery, cook for 2 minutes. Add thyme and wine and turn up heat. Reduce sauce by half, add duck stock and reduce by half again. Add duck meat. Turn down heat and simmer for 2–3 minutes.

Assembly

Remove ravioli from water and drain well, add to duck ragù and toss together until pasta is completely coated in sauce. Season with salt and black pepper to taste. Spoon mixture between four large pasta bowls. Garnish with chopped parsley, crispy duck skin, shaved Parmesan and drizzle with truffle oil.

Coppi

DEANES AT QUEENS

CHRIS FEARON

DEANES AT QUEENS: CHRIS FEARON

Deanes at Queens and Chef Chris Fearon are a culinary match made in heaven as both proudly wear their heart on their sleeve. Chris does it literally by indelibly declaring his passion for food with a striking fine art tattoo on his forearm depicting a plump pumpkin, vibrant beetroot and shimmering seafood nestled in swirling verdant foliage. Poised before his flaming charcoal oven with his sleeves rolled up ready for action, it's clear 35-year-old Chris is earthy, honest and strong. And so is his approach to cooking. By contrast, the cool, restrained architecture and informal bar/grill set-up of this contemporary restaurant provide the perfect contrasting backdrop for Chris's powerful, uplifting and flavourful dishes.

Discreetly positioned in front of the gothic architecture of Queen's University and Methodist College, Deanes at Queens brings a relaxed, all-day continental-style eating experience to Belfast's famous district of saints and scholars. Owned by pioneering chef and restaurateur Michael Deane, this vibrant bistro is the least formal in his impressive portfolio of eating establishments. The food is invitingly familiar but lifted by inspired complementary taste combinations that elevate it to the sublime. Despite the informality of the dining ambiance, quality and flavour are never compromised. The flexible menu changes to reflect what's in season, underpinning a commitment to use the best fresh ingredients available. So Peppered Monkfish and Braised Oxtail are served with Fondant Potatoes,

Glazed Honey Shallots and Black Garlic, while Mourne Lamb and Braised Shoulder are accompanied by BBQ Red Pepper, Parmesan Polenta, Date and Cumin. It's traditional food with a flavour twist that dials it up to special.

At Deanes at Queens, standards are set from the top, and they are set very high. As well as owning a string of successful and respected restaurants around the city centre, Michael Deane held a Michelin star for 13 years – the longest ever in Ireland. As a leading pioneer of the great Belfast food renaissance, he has significantly contributed to putting Belfast firmly on the European food map. He has mentored and nurtured many young chefs that have gone on to make their unique contributions to the local restaurant culture. All of them are exceptionally confident and competent and are testament to the quality of their teacher.

So in 2008, when Michael wanted a rising star to head up his kitchen in Deanes at Queens, he turned to Chris Fearon. Both chefs share a passion for big flavours based on local, simple, hearty food prepared to perfection. Chris is proud of his local roots, and he used his 2011 winning appearance on the BBC Great British Menu to showcase not just his extensive talents, but also champion the best produce Northern Ireland has to offer in a typically down-to-earth way. Michael Deane's faith in Chris has paid off. Under his leadership, the restaurant has been awarded a Michelin Bib Gourmand and 2AA Rosettes and is always popular with the city's diners.

Chris grew up in the beautiful seaside village of Warrenpoint in the shadow of the Mourne Mountains. He started, as many chefs do, washing dishes at a local restaurant, and this experience in a professional kitchen piqued his interest in cooking, so he progressed to catering college. After receiving his basic training, he went to work at 4AA Rosettes Nuremore Hotel with Raymond McArdle for two years. After taking a year to work in restaurants in Australia, his career began in earnest when he joined the team at Shu on Belfast's Lisburn Road. For the next six years under Chef Brian McCann, he learned the ethos of using good, fresh ingredients presented simply.

Chris has evolved his unique cooking style over his eight years heading up the kitchen in Deanes at Queens. His dishes are on one level simple and hearty, the food he readily admits he likes to eat. But the thought process behind the design of his dishes is deceptively complex. He has used his vast experience and natural ability to combine subtle flavours, singing in harmony to make deliciously memorable dishes. He believes you have to keep it simple and get the basics exactly right. Like Chris himself, his food is plain speaking and his earthy flavour combinations appeal to primal human instincts. He refuses to be pigeonholed into a particular style of cooking, but he loves to take traditional Irish dishes and prepare them using classic French techniques to allow the ingredients to be reimagined and tasted anew.

HAM HOCK & SMOKED CHICKEN TERRINE, PICKLES AND SALAD CREAM

Serves 10

Terrine

3 or 1½kg ham hocks
1 large leek
2 smoked chicken breasts
1 large carrot
6 asparagus spears
4 button onions
1 leaf gelatine
100ml good brown chicken stock

Salad Cream

1 tbsp plain flour
4 tsp sugar
1 tbsp English mustard
2 whole eggs
100ml white wine vinegar
150ml double cream
lemon juice
salt

Pickled Vegetables

1 fresh beetroot, thinly sliced
1 peeled cucumber, sliced into
    ½ inch discs
1 peeled carrot, sliced into ribbons
4 button onions, peeled
1 cauliflower, broken into florets
4 firm plums, stoned and sliced
    into wedges
250ml white wine vinegar
250ml white wine
250ml apple juice
150g caster sugar

Method

1. Cover ham hocks in cold water in a large pot, cover with a lid and cook for 3 hours on a medium heat. Break ham hocks down by removing the meat off the bone and break into small chunks. Remove any fat left on the hocks and set aside for later. **2.** Blanch all the vegetables in salty boiling water until tender then refresh in iced water. Set aside for later. **3.** Dice the cooked smoked chicken, set aside. **4.** Heat the stock and soak the gelatine in cold water. When the gelatine is soft, add the leaf to the hot stock and set aside. **5.** To assemble the terrine, line the mould with cling wrap, then cover the base with cooked ham hock meat followed by the chicken and then scatter the mixed vegetables over the meat. Press down the mix to help the terrine stay together when served. Repeat this process until the terrine is full, then gently fill with stock. Place into the fridge overnight to set. **6.** For the Salad Cream, mix the eggs, mustard, flour and sugar together in a heatproof bowl. Heat the vinegar and pour into the egg mix. Set the bowl over a pot of hot water and whisk the egg mix until thick. Fold in the cream, season with lemon juice and salt and place into the fridge to chill.

7. For the Pickled Vegetables, place all the vegetables and plums in a large preserving jar and leave to one side. To make the pickle, place all liquid and sugar in a pot and bring to the boil. Take off the heat and leave until the liquid is cold. Pour the cold pickle into the jar making sure the vegetables are covered, close the lid on the jar and leave for 1 week before eating.

Assembly

Serve as shown.

Deanes at Queens

ROAST SQUAB PIGEON, HEART & LIVER PASTILA, DUKKAH BURNT CABBAGE AND ROMESCO

Serves 2

Core Ingredients

1 squab pigeon,
 weighing 300–500g

Pastila

4 sheets feuille de brick pastry
heart and liver from 1 squab pigeon
1 shallot, finely diced
½ clove garlic, minced
50g pitted prunes
25g golden raisins
½ tsp ground cinnamon
1 ground clove
½ tsp grated ginger
10ml argan oil
25g flaked almonds
100g butter
icing sugar for dusting

Dukkah Burnt Cabbage

110g hazelnuts, finely chopped
80g sesame seeds
2 tbsp coriander seeds
2 tbsp cumin seeds
2 tsp black pepper
1 tsp pink peppercorns
25g pistachio nuts
1 hispi sweet heart cabbage
1 tbsp peanut oil

Romesco

100g whole almonds
100ml rapeseed oil
100g fresh breadcrumbs
30g smoked paprika
3 cloves garlic
1 pinch saffron
8 tomatoes
2 red peppers
1 red chilli
1 lemon

Method

1. First cut the legs off the pigeon and set aside, leaving just the crown with the breasts attached. Remove the liver and heart from inside the carcass of the crown. Place the crown of the pigeon and the legs in a warm pan and cook for 2 minutes on each side. Add 100g of butter into the pan and spoon the melted foaming butter over the carcass, set aside. **2.** Place the roasted legs and crown into a preheated oven at 200°C and roast for 8 minutes, allow to rest the meat for 10–12 minutes before carving the breasts off the crown and serving. **3.** For the Pastila, chop the removed hearts, liver, shallots, ginger and garlic. Gently cook in a large pan on a medium heat with 50g butter. After 5 minutes remove from the pan and set aside. **4.** Chop the raisins, prunes and in a large bowl add the clove, cinnamon and argan oil, then add the liver and hearts mix to the bowl and season well with salt and pepper. **5.** Butter the pastry sheets with a brush and place another sheet of pastry on top, fill with the mix and roll into a cigar shape making sure the sides are sealed. Brush again with butter and sprinkle with almonds and icing sugar. Place the pastila into the fridge to firm for 20 minutes. **6.** Bake the pastila in a preheated oven at 160°C for 16 minutes until golden and crisp. **7.** For the Dukkah Burnt Cabbage, place all the dukkah mix in a food processor and blend on the highest setting for 20 seconds. Put onto an oven tray and bake at 160°C for 8 minutes, remove and allow to cool.

8. Cut the cabbage into ¼, cutting through the root of the cabbage so it stays together. Brush with oil and press into the dukkah mix on all sides. **9.** Place a heavy griddle pan on a high heat and after 10 minutes cook the cabbage allowing it to burn and blacken on all sides, when this is done the cabbage will be cooked. **10.** For the Romesco, roast almonds in the oven at 160°C for 12 minutes until golden brown, set aside. **11.** Chop the tomatoes, chilli and red peppers in half and season, place on an oven tray and bake at 160°C for 45 minutes until slightly blackened and soft, set aside. **12.** Place the garlic, saffron and oil in a small pot and heat to 60°C, set aside to infuse. **13.** In a food processor, blend all the ingredients, the almonds, tomatoes, peppers and the infused oil together, then add the breadcrumbs and lastly season with lemon juice, salt and pepper to taste. Serve at room temperature.

Assembly

Serve as shown.

CHOCOLATE TRUFFLE, RASPBERRY RUFFLE, HAZELNUTS AND SORBET

Serves 12

Chocolate Truffle
400g dark 70% chocolate
500g whipping cream
120g glucose syrup
120g water
120g sugar

Raspberry Ruffle Base
330g coconut flakes
130g condensed milk
330g raspberry purée

Raspberry Sorbet
30g glucose syrup
20g caster sugar
50ml water
200g raspberry purée
3g super neutrose stabiliser

Roast Hazelnuts
100g glucose syrup
100g hazelnuts
60g sugar

Method

1. Whisk the cream until soft peaks, set into the fridge until later. 2. Melt the chocolate in a bowl over a pot of hot water. 3. Place the water, glucose and sugar in a pot and bring to the boil over a gentle heat. Pour over melted chocolate and fold in the cream, set aside. 4. Mix the coconut flakes, condensed milk and raspberry purée together in a bowl, empty into a 12" round flan ring case then pour over the chocolate mix. Set into the fridge to set for 3 hours. 5. For the Raspberry Sorbet, place all liquid in a pot and bring to the boil, add super neutrose, pass through a sieve and allow to cool. 6. Place the mix into an ice cream machine and churn until frozen. Put in the freezer. 7. For the Roast Hazelnuts, place the glucose and sugar in a pot and heat. Mix in the nuts then spread flat on a baking sheet and bake in an oven at 160°C for 12 minutes until golden brown.

Assembly

Run a blow torch around the flan ring to release the chocolate. Slice the chocolate truffle with a hot knife and use a hot ice cream scoop to spoon on the sorbet. Sprinkle with chopped hazelnuts.

Deanes at Queens

DEANES EIPIC

DANIELLE BARRY

DEANES EIPIC: DANIELLE BARRY

Aged just 30, Chef Danielle Barry is universally recognised as a rising star in Belfast's culinary firmament. Her interstellar trajectory started in a very down-to-earth way growing up on a farm in Mayobridge, Co. Down. Despite her tender years, Danielle's precocious journey began when preparing lunches for farm workers on the family farm. Recently, she celebrated becoming one of an elite group of female Michelin-starred chefs – only the second female chef ever in Ireland to gain a star.

From the outset, Danielle has never been afraid to roll up her sleeves and get her hands dirty. She started at the bottom of the ladder washing pots in a local restaurant to earn pocket money and realised she enjoyed the energy of a busy kitchen. At 16, she knew she wanted to be a chef and opted to leave school halfway through her A-Levels to attend catering college. Armed with core competencies and a natural talent, her work experience placement at Deanes in 2003 turned into a permanent position when Chef Michael Deane recognised her potential. Four years training and experience in Deane's Michelin-starred restaurant furnished her with an excellent grounding in classic techniques and disciplined presentation.

Aged 20, Danielle wanted not to just see the world but to taste the world. She took her kitchen skills and embarked on an adventure to expand her culinary repertoire and life experiences. Her travels took her to South Africa, Australia, New Zealand, Spain and then Cumbria in England.

With each step, Danielle soaked up the atmosphere, flavours and cooking techniques of different cultures and added them to her personal book of taste reference points. Exposure to global fusion cuisine at the highest level sparked her imagination and palate and helped raise her to a new degree of professionalism.

The high-level discipline essential for winning a Michelin star came when she returned to the UK to work with pioneering Chef Simon Rogan of L'Enclume restaurant. Working in a two Michelin-star kitchen, Danielle learned a new respect for food provenance. She fell back on her childhood experiences growing up in the Mourne Mountains to go foraging in local forests and coastlines for in-season, local produce like samphire, wild garlic and sloe berries. Inspired by a Scandinavian ethos towards nature, Danielle incorporated deep, fresh, native flavours into her food to create innovative, modern dishes built on flavour. Impressed with Danielle's enthusiasm and application, Simon appointed her Head Chef of his other Cumbrian restaurant, Rogan and Co, where she served for two and a half years.

Michael Deane was monitoring his young protégé's reputation for excellence from afar. In 2015, he was ready to launch his new eatery, Eipic (Irish for Epic). There was a lot invested in this project – financially and psychologically. Eipic was Michael's ambitious bid to win back the Michelin star he had previously held from 1997 to 2010. It was lost after his flagship restaurant suffered

a devastating flood and was forced to close temporarily. But never one to lie down under adversity, Michael came back stronger opening Deanes Hub incorporating Love Fish, The Meat Locker and Eipic in Belfast city centre. Michael persuaded Danielle to come home to head up Eipic. He wanted a natural talent who could achieve the delicate balance of creating innovative but accessible food in a sophisticated but unpretentious setting. Danielle embodied all those qualities. With control over the inspired tasting menu, featuring simple but magnificent dishes like Field Mushrooms with Wild Garlic and Chestnut Pasta or Rhubarb, Sorrel Yoghurt with Iced Rosehip Tea, within 18 months, Danielle and her team had netted that elusive Michelin star.

Danielle's food is consistently inventive and flavour-driven. She uses her classical training to liberate the flavours and textures of fresh produce in a way to invigorate even the most jaded palate. Her sleeves remain rolled up as she continues to spend her free time foraging the bounty of local nature to feature in her food. Danielle Barry's Michelin star is a shining beacon of inspiration for Belfast's next generation of up-and-coming chefs. She has quietly, but confidently, proved what's achievable through application and dedication. Her commitment to excellence, passion for local ingredients and attention to detail is already raising the bar for the city's restaurant scene. With talent of this calibre currently working in Belfast, the future looks deliciously exciting for foodies.

CHARRED MONKTAIL, CREAMED AND PICKLED KOHLRABI, ROAST BONE SAUCE AND COASTAL GREENS

Serves 4

Monkfish
2 small monkfish tails,
    225–250g
500ml water
50g beurre noisette
    (brown butter)
5g salt

Creamed Kohlrabi
2 kohlrabi
200ml cream
100ml milk
2 knobs butter

Pickled Kohlrabi
1 kohlrabi
150ml white wine vinegar
75g sugar
75ml water

Coastal Greens
sea beets
sea purslane
sea asters

Roast Bone Sauce
600g fish bones
1 leek
1 stick celery
1 onion
1 clove garlic
1 litre white fish stock
50g butter

Method

1. To prepare the monkfish, remove any skin or sinew from the outside, keeping on the bone. A fishmonger will do this. **2.** Boil 500ml water, add the salt and allow to cool completely. Submerge the monk tails in this seasoned water when cold for 10 minutes. Afterwards rinse in cold water and pat dry. Place the monk tails into one vacuum pouch each, add 25g beurre noisette to each bag and seal tight. **3.** Cook in a water bath set at 48°C for 12 minutes. Remove and rest on a tray to be finished with a blow torch for charred effect. Alternatively, cook on a barbecue turning the monkfish every 2 minutes for 8 minutes. **4.** For the Pickled Kohlrabi, peel and cut the kohlrabi in half using a mandolin slice lengthways to get even thin slices, they should be floppy. Cut to the desired shape. Keep any trim for the creamed kohlrabi. **5.** Bring the vinegar, sugar and water to the boil and allow to cool slightly. Drop the sliced kohlrabi in and allow to sit for at least 10 minutes. **6.** For the Creamed Kohlrabi, peel and chop the kohlrabi into similar sized slices to ensure even cooking. Place in a saucepan with the milk and cream and cook for 15 minutes until the kohlrabi breaks down. Transfer to a blender and purée until smooth, adding the butter. Season to taste.

7. To make the Roast Bone Sauce, roast the bones in an oven at 200°C until a deep golden colour. Chop the vegetables into small dice and cook in a saucepan until soft and coloured, stirring every few minutes to prevent burning. Add the bones and cover with the white fish stock. Bring to the boil and simmer for 25 minutes. **8.** Pass through a sieve into a clean saucepan and boil on a high heat until reduced by two thirds. When reduced, whisk in the butter until it thickens or use a hand blender.

Assembly

Warm the creamed kohlrabi and dot onto the plate. Pour a pool of the sauce into the middle of the plate. Finish the monkfish with a chef's blow torch to create a charred colour and season. Remove the fillets from the bone and place a fillet on each plate. Place the pickled kohlrabi slices around the fish and finish with coastal herbs tossed in warm butter. Alternatively, samphire works as a substitute for the coastal greens.

Deanes Eipic

CHESTNUT PASTA, WILD GARLIC CREAM AND CHESTNUT MUSHROOMS

Serves 4

Chestnut Pasta
200g strong flour
135g chestnut flour
3 whole eggs
2 tbsp olive oil
pinch salt

Wild Garlic Cream
2 shallots
1 clove garlic
200ml chicken stock
200ml cream
3 large handfuls wild garlic leaves
1 tbsp chopped parsley

Chestnut Mushrooms
8 chestnut mushrooms
1 shallot
1 garlic
50ml cream
2 knobs butter

Method

1. For the Chestnut Pasta, place the dry ingredients in a bowl, make a well in the centre, add the eggs and olive oil and mix together to form a dough. Knead for 5 minutes, wrap in cling film and allow to rest for 20 minutes before rolling. 2. Using a pasta machine, roll the dough into a thin sheet, starting at the highest setting and reducing until you reach the lowest/thinnest setting. You can flour the pasta and bench to prevent sticking. Cut the pasta to your desired shape or use a medium round cutter and pinch the middle to create a fold. Allow to dry at room temperature for 1 hour or keep fresh in the fridge covered with a damp cloth. 3. For the Wild Garlic Cream, finely slice the shallots and garlic, place in a saucepan with the chicken stock and reduce by half. Add the cream and reduce by half again. When cream is reduced add all the chopped wild garlic and chopped parsley. Stir in until wilted and transfer to a blender to purée. Season. 4. For the Chestnut Mushrooms, dice the garlic and shallots and cook on a high heat with one knob of butter until soft. Add the chestnut mushrooms (quartered) and colour. Add the cream and second knob of butter, bring to the boil and remove from heat.

Assembly

Blanch the pasta in boiling salted water for 4 minutes if dried and 2 minutes if fresh. Mix the pasta into the pan with the creamy mushroom sauce. Arrange the pasta into bowls, garnish with fresh wild garlic leaves, flowers and grated chestnuts. Pour the wild garlic cream around.

SUKI RED BERRY TEA CAKE, RHUBARB SORBET AND ICED SORREL

Serves 4

Tea Cake
200g plain flour
14g baking powder
1g salt
30g caster sugar
zest 2 lemons
50g Suki red berry tea leaves
3 eggs
145g honey
30ml milk
1 tin condensed milk
120g melted butter

Rhubarb Sorbet
500g rhubarb stalks
60g sugar
zest 1 orange
15ml rose water
100ml water

Rhubarb Purée
200g rhubarb stalks
45g sugar

Iced Sorrel
300g sheep sorrel
300g water
80g sugar

White Chocolate Powder
120g malto
90g white chocolate

Method

1. For the Tea Cake, warm the milk, honey, condensed milk and dried tea together in a saucepan. Whisk the eggs, sugar and lemon zest until light and fluffy. Add the tea and milk mixture to this then fold in the dry ingredients to form a thick batter. Pour into a standard medium cake tin lined with greaseproof and cook at 170°C for 15–20 minutes. It should be springy to touch and a skewer should come out clean.
2. To make the Rhubarb Sorbet, cut the rhubarb into 6cm pieces, place in a pan and cover with the water, sugar, orange zest and rose water and cook over a medium heat until the rhubarb softens. Transfer to a blender and purée until smooth, place in a freezer and stir every 15 minutes until frozen. **3.** For the Rhubarb Purée, chop the 200g rhubarb into thin slices and coat with sugar. Put into a hot pan and cook quickly over a high heat, stirring continuously until it has all broken down. Purée until smooth in a blender or pass through a sieve.
4. For the Iced Sorrel, bring the sugar and the water to the boil and blend with the sorrel (if unavailable, use basil). Pass through a sieve and place into the freezer. Every 15–20 minutes, stir the mixture with a fork to create an iced granita.
5. For the White Chocolate Powder, melt the white chocolate and whisk in the malto.

Assembly

Slice the tea cake, place the rhubarb sorbet on top and dot the purée around. Spoon over the iced sorrel and white chocolate powder.

Deanes Eipic

GENERAL MERCHANTS

TIM FETHERSTON

GENERAL MERCHANTS: TIM FETHERSTON

General Merchants is 34-year-old Chef Tim Fetherston's first eatery in Belfast. Located in the east of the city, on the outer boundary of a now flourishing restaurant scene, General Merchant's location reflects the personality of its owner and chef. Here you can shamelessly enjoy cooked-to-order breakfast right up to 5pm. Or slope in at 6pm and embrace the heartwarming evening menu featuring dishes such as 48-hour marinated Lamb Shoulder served with Lebanese Flatbread or Portavogie Prawn and Asparagus Risotto.

Tim's food ethos is relaxed and confident with a lightness of touch that belies his passion and attention to detail when it comes to ingredients and presentation. As a millennial youth, he draws influences from the music and epic cinema of that era – the sort where the underdog always triumphs. He is driven by a restless curiosity that has taken him working and travelling all over the world. Not necessarily in pursuit of an end goal, but simply for the exhilarating experience of life itself. That vital life force is apparent in his dishes.

While General Merchants, opened in 2015 with the support of his partners Curt Wigham and Sam Alexander from 5A Café in Stranmillis, is ostensibly designated as a café, a quick glance at Tim's menu tells you it's much more.

The food on offer is rustic, honest and playful, clearly drawing inspiration from the chef's own life experiences.

Tim believes the enjoyment of food is primal – it's our first experience of the expression of love. This is a concept he takes seriously, as evidenced by his thoughtful combinations of flavours and textures.

His fondest childhood food memory is making Fifteens tray bakes at primary school. Three decades later, like a Proustian memory, those Fifteens re-emerge on his menu, deconstructed then reconstructed into moreish Belgian waffles with digestive crumble, condensed caramel milk, cherry jus, toasted marshmallows and toasted coconut.

His savoury offerings are also coy, seductive invites to primal sensory pleasure. Slow-cooked Cannellini Beans enrobed in Passata, Maple Syrup, Cumin and Paprika, jostle for attention with Homemade Corn Fritters topped with Avocado, Poached Egg, Sumac and Bacon. Tim's Melbourne Breakfast, an homage to his ten years living and working in Australia, combines a heady mix of ingredients including vegemite, smashed avocado and capers – all topped with a soft poached egg.

A native of County Down, Tim's culinary journey started in early childhood at his mother's East Belfast café where he worked for pocket money but with no obvious passion for the craft.

It wasn't until he went to Edinburgh aged 18 and began working in the kitchen of the elegant Caledonian Hotel, where he was taken under the wing of top chefs, that he realised he could make it his career and strive for greatness. With each subsequent step of his culinary journey through some of the world's most innovative cafés, pubs, hotels and restaurants, Tim has absorbed influences and inspirations that are now infused in his lively, but laid-back cooking style.

Now settled back in Belfast, Tim opens a new chapter in the story of the city's bustling food scene. His passion and talent are highlighting the culinary opportunities at the inner city boundaries. Tim Fetherston can be confident in the knowledge that with food this good, patrons will enthusiastically seek him out.

MELBOURNE SWEETCORN FRITTERS

Serves 4

Fritter Mix

2 corn cobs
3 large free range eggs
1 tsp strong Dijon mustard
1 cup Clandeboye yoghurt
1 tbsp full fat milk
2 cups rice flour
1 tsp baking powder
1 tbsp ground cumin
1 tsp turmeric
1 pinch nutmeg
1 tsp sumac

Core Ingredients

30g Ballymaloe Relish
    or decent substitute
½ avocado scooped from its shell
seed mix of linseed, pumpkin
    and sesame
salt and pepper
Broighter Gold liquid gold oil
1 punnet mustard cress
1 bunch flat leaf parsley
2 rashers good quality maple
    cured bacon
1 poached egg

Method

1. Place corn on chopping board and slice off the kernels with a knife. **2.** Place flour, baking powder and spices into a large plastic bowl. Add a good pinch of sea salt and cracked pepper. **3.** In a separate bowl, crack the three eggs, add the mustard, yoghurt and milk. Whisk until a smooth batter is formed. Add the rice flour and spice mix and whisk until smooth. Add the sweetcorn to the mix and fold in with a spatula. **4.** Pick the leaves off the parsley and with a knife chop the parsley until fine. Add the parsley to the mix and fold until even. **5.** Cook bacon under a hot grill to your liking. **6.** Place two heaped tablespoons of the fritter mix into an oiled, medium-hot, non-stick frying pan. Cook for 3 minutes or until the bottom is golden brown and crisp. Flip fritter with fish slice and cook for another 3 minutes. **7.** Poach your egg in a pot with a touch of white vinegar for 2–4 minutes.

Assembly

Smear Ballymaloe Relish onto a plate of choice. Place scooped avocado onto the plate and season well. Stack the fritters on top of each other beside the avocado. Top fritters with grilled bacon and the poached egg. Sprinkle some sumac and the three-seed mix on top, and place some mustard cress around the plate. Finish with Broighter Gold rapeseed oil.

General Merchants

TURKISH GÖZLEME

Serves 4–6

Pickled Red Cabbage
1 red cabbage
2 litres water
⅓ cup caster sugar
¾ cup white wine vinegar
5 bay leaves
⅓ cup table salt
1 pricked chilli

Gözleme Dough
200g plain flour
20g melted butter
1 pinch salt
⅓ tsp baking powder
100ml water

Lamb Mince Filling
2 tbsp vegetable oil
500g lamb mince
1 tsp garlic purée
1 tsp ground cumin
½ tsp sumac
½ tsp smoked paprika
salt and pepper to season
2 tbsp pomegranate molasses
1 tsp chopped fresh lemon thyme
1 small block grated feta cheese
1 handful pomegranate seeds
1 tbsp tri-seed mix
Broighter Gold rapeseed oil
1 bunch flat leaf parsley

Sautéed Spinach
400g baby spinach leaves
1 chilli, thinly sliced
salt and pepper

Hummus
3 cups cooked chickpeas
1 garlic clove, puréed
350g tahini paste
140ml lemon juice
3 tbsp olive oil
4 tbsp water
salt and pepper to season

Method

1. For the Gözleme Dough, place flour, baking powder and salt into a food processor. Turn on and pour in water and melted butter. A dough should form. Take out and leave in fridge to rest for at least 1 hour. **2.** For the Pickled Red Cabbage, slice red cabbage thinly on mandolin and place into a large bowl. Meanwhile place water, vinegar, sugar, salt, bay leaves and a chilli pricked with a fork into a pot and bring to the boil. Pour the gastrique onto the cabbage and leave for at least 5 hours to pickle. Portion and cool in the fridge. **3.** For the Sautéed Spinach, add vegetable oil to a pan on a medium heat and sauté the spinach, season and add chilli. When wilted transfer to some kitchen roll and pat to remove the excess liquid. **4.** For the Lamb Mince Filling, in another pan add vegetable oil and turn on to high heat. Add the lamb mince and cook for 2 minutes. Add garlic and and thyme and cook for a further 2 minutes. Add all the spices and the molasses and cook for a further 12 minutes on a low heat. Season. Transfer to container and allow to cool. **5.** For the Hummus, process the salt and garlic together in a food processor. Add the chickpeas and blend until smooth, gradually adding the tahini, lemon juice and water. Stop the processor every now and then and scrape down the side to mix evenly. Add the oil and season to taste. Transfer to container and put aside. **6.** Take a 40g ball from the gözleme dough and roll out with a pinch of flour to form a 9 inch pizza style dough. It should be thin but not transparent.

Place this in a large non-stick frying pan with a little oil on a medium heat. On one half of the dough place 150g lamb mince, a good pinch of feta cheese and some of the spinach. It should be evenly distributed. After 2 minutes fold the dough on top of the mix like a calzone (filled pizza). Cook in the oven at 180°C for 7 minutes. **7.** Take a large handful of cabbage and give a good squeeze to remove any excess pickling juice. Place in a kitchen bowl and add a good pinch of pomegranates, chopped flat leaf parsley, some seed mix and season.

Assembly
On a plate make a smear with the hummus. Place the pickled cabbage salad on the side. Cut the gözleme into triangles and stack on top of each other. Sprinkle with sumac, seeds, pomegranates, sea salt and a good lug of olive oil. Serve immediately.

SOUTHERN STYLE PULLED PORK EGGS BENEDICT

Serves 6

Core Ingredients

2kg pork shoulder or neck
1 smoked ham hock
2 eggs per person
1 cup sliced spring onions

Rub

230g soft brown sugar
85g paprika
1½ tbsp smoked paprika
1 tbsp chilli flakes
2 tbsp ground cumin
½ tbsp salt
½ tbsp cracked pepper
1 tbsp toasted fennel seeds

Sauce

½ cup brown sugar
½ cup cider vinegar
1 cup tomato ketchup
1 tbsp smoked paprika
1½ litres chicken stock

Hollandaise Sauce

6 egg yolks
400g salted butter, melted
1 tbsp cider vinegar
½ cup chopped chives
1 tsp lemon juice
salt and pepper to season

Jalepeño Cornbread

½ brown onion, finely diced
2 jalepeño chillies, finely diced
3 cups corn meal/polenta will do
2 cups plain flour
½ cup caster sugar
3 tbsp baking powder
1 pinch salt
1 pinch black pepper
3 cups buttermilk
½ cup melted butter
3 whole eggs
1 egg white
3 tsp vegetable oil

Method

1. Combine the dry rub ingredients together in a bowl. Place the pork shoulder and hock into the mix and rub all over. Place the ham hock onto an oven tray first and then lay the pork shoulder on top. Cover with baking paper and double tin foil and bake in the oven at 160°C for 1½ hours. Reduce the temperature to 120°C and cook for another five hours. **2.** After 30 minutes resting the pork, pour the meat liquor from your roasting pan through a sieve into a medium-sized kitchen pot and turn on to a medium heat. In a separate mixing bowl, whisk the sauce ingredients together and pour them into the hot meat liquor. Reduce sauce to one third of original size. **3.** When the meat is cooler, pick through and pull it apart into chunks. Get rid of any excess fat or bones from the ham hocks. Place in a container and pour and mix the reduced sauce in until well combined. Place in fridge to cool. **4.** Finely dice the onion and jalepeños. Make a dry mix with the corn meal, flour, sugar, baking powder, salt, pepper, onions and jalepeños. Make a wet mix with the buttermilk, eggs and melted butter by whisking together. In a separate bowl, whisk the egg white until stiff peaks are formed. Fold the wet mix into the dry mix until incorporated and then fold the egg white in gently, trying to leave some air in the mix. **5.** Line two rectangular baking tins with greaseproof paper on the bottom and pour in the batter. Preheat your oven to 180°C and place the bread inside for 35 minutes.

Check the centre of the bread with a wooden skewer (if the mix is still wet on the skewer), rotate the bread 180 degrees and bake for another 12 minutes. Take out and leave to rest for 15 minutes. Flip bread onto a wire rack and let it cool down naturally. **6.** Place six egg yolks into a metal bowl. Add the cider vinegar and place bowl on top of a kitchen pot half filled with simmering water. Whisk the eggs for around 3 minutes vigorously. The sabayon should triple in size. When there is thick ribbons, add the melted butter while whisking. Add the lemon juice, seasoning and chives.

Assembly

Place desired amount of the pork mix into a pan and heat until simmering. Meanwhile place a medium-sized kitchen pot on stove with water and add a couple of tablespoons of white vinegar. Slice cornbread two fingers thick and grill until golden brown on both sides. Crack two large free range eggs into your poaching pot and cook for 2–4 minutes. Place cornbread in centre of plate. Top with the hot pork mix. Carefully place eggs on top of the pork mix. Nappe your hollandaise onto each egg. Top with sliced scallions or mustard cress. Serve with fresh orange juice or a Bloody Mary.

General Merchants

GRAZE

JOHN MOFFATT

GRAZE: JOHN MOFFATT

The district of Ballyhackamore, located in East Belfast, has developed as a real foodie destination in the last few years. So many excellent eateries have sprung up on both sides of the road in this urban village that locals have given it the affectionate moniker 'Ballysnackamore'. One of those outstanding restaurants, Graze, has already built up a loyal customer base. It's home to owner/Chef John Moffatt and his business partner Neil Johnston. Thirty-four-year-old Chef John Moffatt grew up in scenic Carrickfergus and spent childhood summers tagging along with his beloved grandfather, a hobby fisherman, who taught him how to prepare freshly caught seafood. He had an outdoor childhood, playing in local fields and foraging for the natural bounty of blackberries and wild garlic. In his formative years, John developed a strong connection to the land and sea and learned the pleasure of food starts with its growing and gathering. His early experiences fostered his love of natural, seasonal food but genetics may have also influenced his career as a chef. His grandmother is a talented artist of direct French descent. One of her paintings of Belfast's iconic giant yellow cranes, Samson and Goliath, hangs pride of place in Graze today. John approaches food with an artist's eye and a chef's palate. He uses a broad spectrum of flavours to create his spectacular food. His sensual plates tell a story of seasonality and how ingredients present in their natural surroundings.

He rejects uniformity and celebrates wildness with organic spiralling tendrils and contrasting colours on the plate.

His kitchen career began at 16 when he started work at a local hotel, although becoming a chef was not a career goal at this point as it was assumed he would follow into the family printing business. This familial heritage perhaps explains why to this day John is so inspired by colour, texture and technical precision. But he quickly realised that being a chef could fulfil his love of food and hospitality and he beat a path to Paul Rankin's Belfast restaurant Cayenne to learn from those at the top of their game. He was mentored by Chef Andy Rea and was schooled in the techniques of classic French cooking. He next moved to Porcelain under the tutelage of Niall McKenna where he learned the rules of modern European cuisine. In 2003, John went to Sydney, Australia, to work and expanded his skills preparing seafood. He worked in The Boathouse, one of the country's best seafood restaurants and relished the daily experience of visiting a vast, local fresh fish market to survey and choose the best catch of the day. John returned to Northern Ireland with new skills and greater maturity in the kitchen. His experience led him to land the Head Chef position at The Bureau, a well-respected gastro pub located in Newtownabbey. During this time, he established strong relationships with local suppliers and began hatching plans to open his own restaurant. At The Bureau, he also met his business partner Neill.

They had the vision to transform an uninspiring office space into an intimate but lively neighbourhood bistro where seasonality and good food are continually celebrated.

Thirty years after his childhood foraging trips, John can still be found gathering wild ingredients to complete his down-to-earth dishes. On his menu, you will discover the best, local, seasonal ingredients accented with homegrown or foraged herbs and greens. Patrons' favourites include the mouth-watering Silverhill Duck Breast served with Spring Leek Potato Cake, Purple Sprouting Broccoli, Peas, Local Rhubarb, Woodland Mushrooms and a Jus; or Hereford Chateaubriand served with Gratin Dauphinoise, Cauliflower, Wild Garlic and Forest Mushrooms. Artistic talent and a French palate are in John Moffatt's DNA and these natural abilities, combined with decades of hard work, equip him to take humble ingredients and transform them into exalted gastronomic masterpieces. At Graze, you will find the artistic offerings not just displayed on the walls, but tantalisingly edible on the plate. As a 'third wave' Belfast chef, John brings passionate energy and a genuine love of food that will further push the boundaries of the city's food culture.

SEARED FOIE GRAS, WHITE ONION VELOUTÉ, BRIOCHE, CHARRED SCALLION, SAUTERNES JELLY, BURNT ONION, TRUFFLE

Serves 1

Core Ingredients
30g escalope foie gras
1 scallion
1 slice brioche
truffle oil
olive oil

Burnt Onion Powder
2 onions
500ml water

White Onion Velouté
100g white onion, finely diced
1 clove garlic, finely diced
1 sprig thyme
1 bay leaf
150ml chicken stock
50ml double cream
salt and pepper

Sauternes Jelly
100ml Sauternes
1 sheet gelatine, immersed
    in cold water for 5 minutes
    until soft then squeezed dry

Method
1. For the Burnt Onion Powder, cut onions in half and place in a roasting tray, pour in water and roast in a very hot oven (215°C) until blackened. Remove the burnt onions and blitz, then place onto a flat tray and spread evenly. Reduce the oven temperature (150°C) and bake the onion mixture for 1 hour to completely dry out. Blitz again adding a pinch of salt and push through a fine sieve to create burnt onion powder. 2. For the White Onion Velouté, gently fry diced onion and garlic with thyme in a little olive oil until translucent, add bay leaf and chicken stock, bring to the boil and then simmer for 5 minutes. Add the cream and bring back to the boil, then simmer for a further 15–20 minutes. Remove the bay leaf, blitz and pass the sauce through a fine sieve, season with salt and pepper. 3. For the Sauternes Jelly, pour Sauternes into a saucepan and bring to the boil, remove from the heat and stir in softened gelatine, pour through a sieve into a mould and refrigerate for 2 hours until set. 4. For the Charred Scallion, blanch scallion in boiling salted water and refresh in iced water before adding to a pan with a little butter. Cook for 1½ minutes until charred on both sides, season with salt, pepper and a squeeze of lemon juice.

Assembly
Sear the foie gras for 1 minute on both sides and place into a hot oven (180°C) for 1½ minutes. Cut the brioche into discs and toast, then cut the Sauternes jelly into 5mm cubes. Place two spoonfuls of white onion velouté onto the centre of a serving plate, set foie gras on top, scatter Sauternes cubes around the plate and arrange brioche discs parallel with the foie gras. Lay the charred scallion on top and season with burnt onion powder and a drizzle of truffle oil before serving.

Graze

TURBOT, GRATIN POTATO, PURPLE SPROUTING BROCCOLI, WILD GARLIC AND PORTAVOGIE PRAWN CHOWDER

Serves 2

Core Ingredients
1 small turbot, filleted
   (keep bones for the sauce)
10g samphire
4 florets purple sprouting broccoli
1 packet micro fennel

Scallop Roe Powder
1 roe, removed from a scallop

Chowder Sauce
turbot bones
1 stick celery, peeled and diced
½ onion, peeled and diced
½ bulb fennel, peeled and diced
2 cloves garlic, peeled and diced
1 tsp lemon juice
½ white leek, washed and diced
500ml milk
200ml single cream
200ml dry white wine
1 bay leaf
3 peppercorns

Chowder
½ carrot, blanched in boiling
   salted water until soft and
   refreshed in salted iced water
½ celery stick
½ leek, finely sliced and diced
50g Portavogie prawns

Potato Gratin
2 large Maris Piper potatoes,
   washed and peeled
200ml milk
200ml double cream
½ onion, diced
2 cloves garlic, peeled and crushed
3 sprigs rosemary
3 sprigs thyme, picked
pinch salt and ground white pepper
5g grated Parmesan

Method
1. For the Scallop Roe Powder, place scallop roe onto a tray, roast in a hot oven (180°C) for 20 minutes before transferring to a dehydrator for 48 hours. Blitz the dried roe in a food processor until it resembles a fine powder. Pass through a fine sieve. **2.** For the Chowder Sauce, chop the turbot bones, add to a saucepan and sweat in a little oil with celery, onion, fennel, garlic, leek and lemon juice, gently cook for 2–3 minutes, add white wine and reduce for 2 minutes before adding milk, cream, a bay leaf and peppercorns, bring to the boil and simmer for 20 minutes. Pass the sauce through a fine sieve and set to the side. **3.** For the Potato Gratin, blitz the milk, double cream, onion, garlic, rosemary, thyme, salt and white pepper together and then pass through a fine sieve. **4.** Finely slice potatoes and add to the mixture, allow to marinate for 30 minutes to absorb flavour. **5.** Layer the slices of potato in a small container, cover with greaseproof paper and tin foil and set into a bain-marie, then place into a hot oven (180°C) and cook for 2 hours 15 minutes. **6.** Remove the potato gratin from its container, set onto a small oven tray and top with Parmesan cheese ready for assembly.

Assembly
Add one teaspoon of oil to a hot pan, season the turbot and place skin side down, cook for 2 minutes before transferring to a hot grill and cook for a further 1½ minutes, remove from the heat and add a little butter, salt, pepper and lemon juice. Place the potato gratin into a hot oven (180°C) and bake until golden brown for 5 minutes. Bring the chowder sauce and vegetables to the boil before adding Portavogie prawns. Place the potato gratin in a serving bowl at 12 o'clock, pour chowder sauce around the base and lay a fillet of turbot on top of the chowder. Garnish with broccoli, wild garlic and samphire. Dust the edge of the plate with the scallop powder, finish with micro fennel and a sprinkle of scallop roe powder.

Graze

WHITE CHOCOLATE AND VANILLA PANNA COTTA, POACHED RHUBARB, MANGO, PISTACHIO AND BLOOD ORANGE SORBET

Serves 2

Core Ingredients

2 rhubarb stalks
1 small blood orange
50g pistachio nuts,
    shelled and peeled
¼ mango, peeled

White Chocolate Cylinder

50g white chocolate

Panna Cotta

280ml double cream
30g icing sugar
1 vanilla pod, cut in half
    lengthways and
    seeds removed
1 sheet gelatine,
    soaked in cold water

Stock Syrup

    (for Sorbet and Rhubarb)
100g caster sugar
200ml water

Blood Orange Sorbet

100ml blood orange juice
50ml stock syrup
½ tsp glucose
½ tsp lemon juice

Method

1. For the Chocolate Cylinder, roll one sheet of acetate width ways and seal with sticky tape to create a one inch tube. Gently melt white chocolate and pour into the cylinder, coating the inside as evenly as possible, tap gently to remove excess chocolate and refrigerate for an hour until set. **2.** For the Panna Cotta, pour cream into a saucepan and bring to the boil with icing sugar, vanilla pod and seeds, reduce the temperature and cook for 5 minutes. Remove from the heat and stir in gelatine before passing through a fine sieve into a dish and refrigerate for 4 hours until almost set. When the panna cotta is almost set, pipe into the chocolate cylinders and return to the fridge. **3.** For the Stock Syrup, pour water into a saucepan and add sugar, bring to the boil and reduce for 5 minutes. **4.** For the Blood Orange Sorbet, pour stock syrup and glucose into a saucepan and bring to the boil, set aside to cool. Add lemon juice and blood orange juice and pour into an ice cream machine and churn until frozen. Store in a freezer. **5.** Wash, top and tail the rhubarb, then peel and place into a deep baking tray. Pour in 150ml stock syrup and bake in a hot oven (180°C) for 9 minutes until tender. Remove the rhubarb from the stock, mash with a fork and strain to remove any excess liquid. **6.** Blitz pistachio nuts in a food processor until they resemble fine crumbs.

7. Peel and segment the blood orange and set aside. **8.** For the Mango Purée, peel and dice mango and place in a small bowl, blitz until smooth and pass through a sieve. **9.** Peel and dice mango and cut into 5mm dice.

Assembly

Sprinkle ground pistachio onto a plate and set the white chocolate cylinder of panna cotta on top, arrange diced mango with mango purée, add segments of blood orange, pistachio nuts, a quenelle of rhubarb and a scoop of blood orange sorbet.

Graze

HADSKIS

CATHAL DUNCAN

HADSKIS: CATHAL DUNCAN

In the last decade, the Cathedral Quarter has become a frenetic hotspot for cultural events, entertainment, food and imbibing. Its labyrinth of interconnected, narrow, cobbled streets makes it an almost vehicle-free oasis of rare, safe urban space. There is laid-back energy conducive to relaxed hospitality and that makes it the perfect home for Chef Cathal Duncan. The softly spoken 30-year-old was appointed Head Chef of Hadskis in 2015 after stints in some of the most respected and fêted eateries in Belfast and London. His calm presence and genial personality make the open kitchen of Hadskis a great stage for Cathal to directly interact with the pulse of patrons' dining demands throughout the day.

Cathal had a nomadic childhood growing up in Dublin, Australia, Galway and Newcastle-upon-Tyne as his parents travelled with work. Back in Ireland in his grandparents' home, he realised the craic was always in the kitchen and a lifelong affection for the camaraderie of shared food was born. In his teenage years, he ignored his Belfast grandmother's advice to avoid the hospitality industry as a career because of the long hours and hard work involved. She was in an expert position to give an opinion as she grafted for 20 years front of house in The Bot – one of Belfast's famously lively student pubs.

His parents encouraged him to get a 'proper' education and he graduated from Queen's University Belfast with a degree in English and History but the lure of the excitement of a professional kitchen proved too much and in 2006 he enrolled in catering college, completing his initial training with a placement in The King's Head gastro pub in South Belfast.

His raw talent and apparent enthusiasm meant he then took a huge step up when he joined the kitchen team at The Merchant Hotel. In one move he went from making very good burgers to prepping truffles and foie gras and his career as a chef began in earnest. After two years learning the ground rules for fine dining at high volume and the importance of consistency of presentation, Cathal went to work in the Michelin-starred Roussillon in Pimlico, Pied à Terre and then Terence Conran's favourite restaurant Boundary in London's trendy Shoreditch. For three years, he worked 85-hour weeks learning new techniques and how to handle the best ingredients available with respect to get the best from them. At Boundary, he was taught by his French mentors how simple food can often be better than complex. In fact, familiar food is a greater challenge because patrons carry their own ideas of how it should taste.

Returning to Belfast in 2013, Cathal realised the development of the city's blossoming restaurant scene and the public appetite for cuisine that pushed the boundaries, joining the groundbreaking team at the newly-opened OX.

This experience further enhanced his understanding of ingredient-led cooking and how the food needs to match the ethos and vision of the restaurant. After a year at OX, he moved to James St. South and became a respected and confident teacher in the Cookery School. After two years, his obvious talents and easy-going nature were recognised by his boss and mentor Chef Niall McKenna. He was promoted within Niall's successful restaurant group to become Head Chef at Hadskis where the flexibility of Cathal's menus makes it very popular with both lunch and evening diners.

Another success story from one of Belfast's top chefs and restaurant entrepreneurs, this narrow, neighbourhood bistro, snuggling along the side of Commercial Court, takes its unusual name from its location. With appropriate synchronicity, Hadskis occupies the former site of an 18th-century foundry where the city's iron pots and pans were once made. Since it opened in 2013, this stylish and minimal linear space has already forged a solid reputation for vibrant food in a casual setting. In this bustling, urban landscape, Hadskis offers a calm haven where you can watch the world in all its exuberant glory go by while indulging in Cathal's home-cooked inspired fare. His food is straightforward and honest, reflecting the understated character of its thoughtful creator.

HADSKIS™

KILKEEL SCALLOPS, CANNELLINI BEANS AND 'NDUJA

Serves 6

Core Ingredients

18 scallops, removed from shell
    and cleaned
250g dried cannellini beans,
    soaked in cold water overnight
100ml vegetable stock
100g 'Nduja
100g butter, diced
2 tbsp vegetable oil
salt, pepper and fresh lemon
    to season
fried brioche breadcrumbs
    and gremolata to serve

Method

1. Place cannellini beans in a pot with plenty of cold water, bring to the boil and skim. Reduce the heat to a gentle simmer and cook until very tender, stirring occasionally. Once cooked season well with salt and allow to cool in the cooking liquor. 2. To finish the beans, bring the vegetable stock to the boil and add the diced butter and 'Nduja. Drain the beans from the cooking liquor and add to the hot sauce. Season with salt, pepper and lemon, keep warm while you cook the scallops. 3. Preheat a non-stick frying pan until very hot, season the scallops with salt and add the vegetable oil to the pan. Carefully place the scallops in the pan and cook for 1 minute, until nicely caramelised. Turn the scallops and cook for a further 30 seconds.

Assembly

Place a small pile of beans and the sauce in the middle of shallow bowls, put the scallops on top. Sprinkle over the brioche crumbs and top with gremolata.

Hadskis

ROAST STONE BASS, HAM HOCK, GREEN LENTILS AND SALSA VERDE

Serves 6

Core Ingredients

6 pieces stone bass fillet,
  approximately 160g each
1 unsmoked ham hock, soaked
  in cold water overnight

Lentils

300g green lentils
2 shallots, finely diced
2 carrots, finely diced
1 small head celeriac,
  finely diced
2 cloves garlic, finely sliced
1 sprig thyme
1 bay leaf
2 litres vegetable stock
100g diced butter
olive oil
salt and pepper

Salsa Verde

4 good quality anchovies,
  finely chopped
1 gherkin, finely chopped
1 tbsp capers, finely chopped
1 clove garlic, finely grated
zest 1 lemon, finely grated
50g flat leaf parsley, finely chopped
20g chives, finely chopped
10g dill, finely chopped
10g mint, finely chopped
1 tsp Dijon mustard
100ml extra virgin olive oil

Method

1. Soak the ham hock in cold water overnight, changing water two or three times. 2. To cook the ham hock, place in a pot with cold water, bring to the boil and skim, reduce the heat and simmer gently for 2–3 hours until tender. Remove the ham from the cooking liquor and allow to cool slightly, pick all the meat off the bone, discarding any fat, skin and bone. Reserve the meat until required. 3. For the Lentils, in a large saucepan sweat diced vegetables in olive oil for 2–3 mins. Add the lentils, garlic, thyme and bay; cover with vegetable stock and bring to the boil. Simmer gently for 10–15 minutes until the lentils are tender. 4. For the Salsa Verde, combine all the ingredients, mix well and taste for seasoning. 5. When the lentils are cooked, drain through a colander reserving 200ml of the cooking liquor to reheat the lentils later. 6. To cook the fish, heat a non-stick frying pan until very hot, season the fish with salt and pepper. Place the fish into the pan skin side down and fry for 2 minutes, then place the pan into a hot oven for 3–4 minutes. 7. Reheat the lentils in the cooking liquor, add the ham hock and the diced butter, cook until the butter has melted and season with salt, pepper and lemon juice.

Assembly

Place the lentils into warmed bowls, top with the fish and plenty of salsa verde.

Hadskis

SPICED RHUBARB POSSET

Serves 6

Core Ingredients

300g fresh rhubarb, chopped
1 large orange, juiced
125g caster sugar
2 lemons, juiced
1 tbsp preserved ginger
    in syrup, finely chopped,
    plus 1 tbsp of the syrup
1 tsp ground cardamom
250ml whipping cream
3 leaves bronze leaf gelatine

Method

1. Boil orange juice and sugar until syrupy, add the rhubarb and cook over a low heat until soft but still intact, remove a third of this mixture for the jelly. The remaining two-thirds, continue to cook until very soft, blend in a food processor until very smooth, reserve and chill. **2.** Strain the rhubarb for the jelly through a fine sieve to extract the liquid. Bloom the gelatine leaves in iced water until soft, bring the rhubarb juice to the boil and squeeze the water out of the gelatine leaves. Whisk the gelatine into the hot rhubarb juice and remove from the heat. Reserve at room temperature. **3.** Bring the cream and lemon juice to the boil, once boiling stir in the rhubarb purée, while warm pour approximately 150ml of the posset mix into serving glasses and chill. **4.** Once the possets have chilled and set carefully, pour a thin layer of the rhubarb jelly on the top (approximately 40ml per glass), return to the fridge to set the jelly.

Assembly

Serve with shortbread biscuits.

Hadskis

HOME

STEPHEN HALLER

HOME: STEPHEN HALLER

The old saying goes 'home is where the heart is' and, in the case of one of Belfast's most vibrant and considered restaurants, that maxim holds true both figuratively and literally. General Manager of Home, 42-year-old Stephen Haller has created a restaurant that cares about its diners in every sense. Home is the manifestation of Stephen's energy and authentic concern to give his customers a positive, healthy food experience in a welcoming space. Nestled close to Belfast's City Hall on Wellington Place, this unique deli and restaurant continually buzzes with energy from early lunch to late dinner. It caters for health-conscious city workers grabbing deli super salads, to families looking for delicious and nutritious affordable dining, to tourists craving a relaxed, authentic Belfast food experience. Everyone is welcome at Home.

Home is a celebration of all things local. Ingredients are sourced fresh directly from the best local artisan bakers and the premier meat, fish and vegetable suppliers. The restaurant's up-cycled furniture offers character to the interior while quirky artwork provides local artists with the opportunity to showcase and sell their work. But the menu is central to the ethos of Home. It's unashamedly packed with healthy dishes based on grains and pulses, made fresh daily and free from preservatives and colourings. Food is prepared with locally-produced, omega-packed rapeseed oil. There are also extensive vegetarian and vegan menus and an impressive selection of gluten-free options.

The up-front deli counter is a tantalising treasure trove of epicurean delights to go. Home's balanced menu includes longstanding favourites like Whipped Goat's Cheese, Beetroot, Apple and Candied Walnuts; Hot and Sour Asian Broth with Chicken, Coriander and Lemongrass; or the taste explosion that is the Salt and Chilli Tofu, Red Pepper Salsa and Saffron Aioli. Home is rightly proud of a healthy, vibrant menu that refuses to compromise on taste or satiety.

That was Stephen Haller's original vision when he opened Home in 2011. It started life as a temporary 'pop-up' restaurant located on a Belfast side street. Working on a micro budget, Stephen wanted to test if there was an appetite for healthy, nutritious, delicious food. The resounding answer from the public was 'yes' and in 2012, Stephen laid down Home's permanent foundations. It's a testament to his intuition and five years later Home is a hive of activity occupying one of the city's most desirable addresses. In 2013, the quality of its food, customer-focused approach and affordable menu were recognised when it was awarded the coveted Bib Gourmand from the Michelin Guide, which it retains to this day.

Home's success must be attributed to Stephen Haller's personal passions and a lifetime's experience on the Belfast restaurant scene. He began his career in 1994, aged 20, at Chef Paul Rankin's legendary Michelin-starred Roscoff in Belfast.

He then went on to be the Assistant Manager of another Belfast Rankin restaurant, Cayenne. With each move, Stephen was learning about the demands of innovative, customer-led cuisine with an emphasis on quality, fresh ingredients. During these years, he formed a firm friendship with Chef Andy Rea. When Andy opened Mourne Seafood Bar in 2006, Stephen became its manager, a crucial role held for five years.

But, like many of the unsung heroes of the hospitality industry, Stephen began to find the intense, hard-working lifestyle impacting negatively on his health. He made a personal commitment to clean up his diet and to improve his overall wellbeing. However, after so many years working in the city's finest restaurants, he was not prepared to compromise on taste, choice or quality – especially when eating out. He also realised he wasn't alone in these demands and many people desire to be able to dine out without compromising their healthy diet. Through this personal experience, he identified a niche in the market fuelled by the zeitgeist for clean eating. Home is his inspired response. With Andy Rea's support and guidance, Stephen's test-bed, pop-up restaurant has flourished to become the place to go in Belfast when you want great-tasting, feel-good food.

SALT AND CHILLI TOFU
WITH MISO SLAW AND VEGAN MAYO

Serves 4

Core Ingredients
2 packets firm tofu
50g rice flour
50g potato flour
nanami togarashi
    (can be found in Asian
    Market) or chilli powder
fine sea salt

Miso Slaw
¼ red cabbage, shredded
1 carrot, grated
4 scallions, chopped
20g coriander, chopped
50g radish, grated
30g pickled ginger, minced

Miso Dressing
3 tbsp siso (wheat free)
3 tbsp soy sauce (wheat free)
3 tbsp sesame oil
1 tbsp toasted sesame seeds
4 tbsp agave or maple syrup
1 lime, juiced
1 lemon, juiced

Asian Vegan Mayo
300g firm tofu
1 tbsp water
1 tbsp lemon juice and
    ¼ zest 1 lemon
5 tsp brown sugar
3 tsp Dijon mustard
1 tbsp olive oil
2 tsp white wine vinegar
¼ cup coriander, chopped
2 tsp curry powder

Method
1. Cut tofu into large dice, cover with flour mix and refrigerate (for best results, do this 1 hour before frying). **2.** Deep fry at highest setting until crispy, remove and season with togarashi and fine sea salt. **3.** For Miso Slaw, mix all ingredients, season with sea salt and dress with Miso Dressing. **4.** For Miso Dressing, mix all ingredients together. **5.** For Asian Vegan Mayo, process all ingredients until smooth. Store in fridge for a few hours to allow flavours to develop and mayo to thicken up. Keeps in fridge for two days.

Assembly
Serve as shown.

CHARGRILLED LAMB LOIN WITH KALE AND QUINOA TABOULEH, SMOKED AUBERGINE AND MINT YOGHURT

Serves 4

Core Ingredients

2 × 350g lamb loins
1 sprig rosemary, chopped
zest ½ lemon
2 garlic, minced
2 tsp sumac
drizzle olive oil

Tabouleh

100g kale leaf, washed and dried
¼ cucumber, finely diced (no seeds)
4 vine ripe tomatoes, finely diced
     (no seeds)
1 pomegranate (seeds only)
4 scallions, finely chopped
1 red chilli, finely chopped
     (optional)
1 lemon – ½ zest, ½ juice
30g parsley
20g mint
1 clove garlic, minced
150g quinoa, cooked
drizzle rapeseed oil

Smoked Aubergine

2 aubergines
2 tbsp tahini
1 lemon, juiced
pinch cayenne pepper
pinch cumin
2 cloves garlic, minced

Mint Yoghurt

100ml Greek yogurt
20g mint leaves

Method

1. Marinate the lamb loins in all of the core ingredients mixed together for 2 hours or overnight. **2.** For Tabouleh, place kale, parsley and mint into a food processor and buzz until finely chopped. Place in a large bowl, add the rest of the ingredients, season with sea salt and pepper and drizzle with rapeseed oil. **3.** For Smoked Aubergine, burn whole aubergine over an open flame, i.e. chargrill or gas burner, until totally burnt on the outside, then pop the aubergine into a hot oven for approximately 10 minutes until the inside of the aubergine is soft. **4.** Remove from the oven, carefully split aubergine, scrape out soft flesh and discard skin. **5.** Place aubergine flesh in a blender with all other ingredients, process until smooth and season with sea salt. **6.** For Mint Yogurt, blend Greek yogurt and mint until smooth.

Assembly

Season lamb with lots of sea salt and cracked black pepper. Place on a hot grill or pan fry. Colour lamb or chargrill on all sides, finish cooking in a hot oven to your liking. Rest lamb for 2 minutes before carving and serving. Serve tabouleh and aubergine at room temperature. Plate as shown.

COCONUT MATCHA PANNA COTTA
WITH INDIAN MANGO AND SESAME FILO COOKIE

Serves 6

Panna Cotta

1 vanilla pod, split and scrape
   vanilla seeds from pod
2 tsp matcha green tea powder
1 lime leaf
½ lemongrass, roughly chopped
225ml coconut milk
200ml whipping cream
½ tin condensed milk
2 gelatine leaves, soaked
   in cold water

Indian Mango

2 Alphonso mango
   or ripe green mangoes

Filo Cookies

3 sheets filo pastry
1 tsp sesame seeds
1 tsp black sesame seeds
caster sugar
50g unsalted butter, melted
2 egg whites mixed together
   with butter

Method

1. In a saucepan, add whipping cream, vanilla, matcha tea, lime leaf and lemongrass. Over a medium heat, bring to a simmer. Simmer for 1 minute then remove from heat. **2.** Remove gelatine from the water, gently squeeze excess water from the gelatine and add to hot cream. **3.** Remove lemongrass, lime leaf, vanilla pod from cream mix. Add condensed milk, coconut milk, buzz mixture with a stick blender for 30 seconds. **4.** Pass mix through a fine sieve and pour into moulds, refrigerate for 6 hours or overnight. **5.** For the Indian Mango, peel mango and cut into neat dice. Process any leftover mango flesh or trim until smooth and mix with diced mango. **6.** For the Filo Cookies, preheat oven to 180°C. **7.** Lay one filo sheet on a baking sheet. Brush filo with butter/egg white mix and then sprinkle with caster sugar. **8.** Lay second filo sheet on top of the first sheet and repeat previous step. Repeat again for the third sheet. The top sheet gets finished with sesame seeds. **9.** Pop tray into the oven. Bake for approximately 8 minutes. Remove from oven and carefully cut/trim filo into long rectangles. Return to the oven and bake until golden, approximately 6 minutes.

Assembly

Heat the outside of the panna cotta mould in hot water to help release, turn onto a plate, spoon round mango and serve cookie on the side. Candied lime and dried coconut optional.

HOWARD STREET

MARTY MURPHY

HOWARD STREET: MARTY MURPHY

Chef Marty Murphy's Howard Street restaurant is Belfast personified. Solid and stocky like a boxer with an artistic side, the welcome is warm but understated. Howard Street is a tension of contradictions that really shouldn't work together, but do. The front doors were salvaged from a Christian Brother's school, while its historic Terrazzo hall floor was an unexpected gift from 19th-century Presbyterians, unearthed during the creation of the interior. And there's the first contradiction – two wonderful elements from different traditions coming together to make something new. This juxtaposition is emblematic of Marty Murphy's approach to cooking. He brings unexpected elements from both Eastern and Western food cultures together and makes them work in concert.

Hailing from West Belfast, the 38-year-old's journey to Chef/owner of Howard Street has been an exciting, if unconventional, one. In the last two decades, Marty has worked as a chef in some of Belfast's most innovative eateries, establishing a good grounding in classic French and modern European cuisine. But his real passion for complex flavours was sparked on an extended trip around South Asia, including attending a cookery school in Thailand. His path to culinary success began simply at 18 years old when he was working as a kitchen porter in Florida. His first glimpse into the magical world of a professional kitchen transfixed him and he immediately fell in love with the intense energy of the chefs.

On return to his native city, he signed up for catering college and approached Michael Deane for a placement. It was a valuable learning period for him when he was schooled in the discipline of what's expected of a Michelin-starred restaurant. After two years, in 2000 he joined the team at Shu on the Lisburn Road. Here, he absorbed a more relaxed and modern style of cooking. To satisfy his youthful wanderlust, he moved to Australia chasing the good life. His introduction to Asian fusion cooking lit a fire within him that burns bright to this day. He is truly passionate about Thai culture and food and has made it his mission to bring the region's authentic flavours to enthusiastic Belfast diners. For example, his popular starter of Spiced Coconut Prawn Soup with Tom Yum, Spring Onion and Coriander is an unfolding revelation of flavour that has become an instant classic. In Australia, he secured a position in the world-famous Sydney Opera House restaurant advancing his skills in French fine dining. That's why you will also find Classic French Onion Soup served with Gruyère Croutons sitting cheek by jowl on his menu with its more exotic companions. Marty's ethos is to give the people what they want – but provide them with the best version of it without the constraint of rigid categorisation.

On returning to Belfast, he worked at James St. South. With such excellent grounding, he was offered the position of Head Chef at Ten Square's Porcelain.

After two successful years at the helm of the boutique hotel's fine dining restaurant, Marty's desire to challenge himself to greater culinary heights lead him to work at the two Michelin-starred Restaurant Vermeer in Amsterdam. The fact he didn't speak a word of Dutch was clearly no barrier to such a fearless chef. Preparation in Restaurant Vermeer was technical and labour intensive and in complete contrast to where he went next – to spend time with indigenous people in South Africa to learn how to marry exotic flavours in harmonious union. This was just one off-the-beaten-track stop on his round-the-world culinary food tour. With every step on his wild gastronomic odyssey, Marty accrued more experience and passion for fusion cooking. He credits his travels with changing the way he thinks about food.

Back in Belfast in 2007, he was appointed Head Chef at Deanes Deli where he had the opportunity to try out his innovative approach to flavour. His next move was to head up the team at the multi-award winning Potted Hen. But Marty refused to be fettered by anyone else's rules and was already fermenting plans to open his own destination restaurant and, in 2013, he opened Howard Street. It reflects the soul of its visionary chef as it speaks to his unique life experiences. Marty is writing his own successful chapter of the Belfast food story and he is doing it in his usual determined way.

SZECHUAN ROAST MONKFISH, BOK CHOI, SPICED CRAB SPRING ROLL AND HOT & SOUR PRAWN BROTH

Serves 2

Core Ingredients
300g monkfish
6 whole bok choi leaves
5g toasted sesame seeds
20g crushed Szechuan pepper

Prawn Broth
50g prawn shells
25g tom yum paste
1 lemongrass stalk, chopped
10g basil stocks
20g shallot, sliced
10g ginger, sliced
1 split red chilli
25ml red wine vinegar
5g grated palm sugar
250ml good quality
    vegetable stock

Spring Roll
2 spring roll wraps
100g fresh white crab meat
    (picked to ensure no
    shell fragments)
20g onion, sliced
20g white cabbage, sliced
10g diced red chilli, deseeded
30g good quality mayonnaise
10ml light soy sauce

Method
1. Ask your local fishmonger to remove the monkfish from bone and remove skin. Cut into two 150g portions and set aside. **2.** For the Prawn Broth, put tom yum paste with a splash of oil onto an oven tray and place in oven at 180°C for 10 minutes until dark red in colour. Roast prawn shells at the same temperature for 10 minutes.
3. In a saucepan gently fry off sliced shallot, lemongrass, basil stalks, ginger and split chilli for 10 minutes, without colouring. Add roasted tom yum paste and cook for a further 10 minutes on a low heat. Add red wine vinegar and palm sugar, reduce to a syrup. Add roasted prawn shells and vegetable stock, simmer for 20 minutes and strain. **4.** For the Spring Roll, in a bowl add picked crabmeat, diced chilli, cabbage, sliced onion, soy sauce and mayonnaise. Mix well until combined. Place spring roll wrapper on a dry surface, take half the crab mix and place it one-third of the way up the wrapper in a rough sausage shape. Tuck in the ends and roll up, sealing the top of the wrap with a little beaten egg.
5. Blanch bok choi in boiling salted water for 1–2 minutes and refresh in iced water.

Assembly
Heat a heavy-based pan and add olive oil. Roll the monkfish in the crushed Szechuan and season with salt. Place fish in pan and cook over a medium heat, turning once or twice before placing in oven at 170°C for 10–12 minutes depending on thickness of fish. Set aside in a warm place. Place broth back on the heat and reduce by one third. Heat a deep fryer to 180°C and cook spring rolls until golden. Remove and cut at an angle. Heat bok choi in broth and add toasted sesame seeds. Arrange in a shallow bowl, with first sliced monkfish, then spring roll. Arrange the bok choi around the spring roll, finally pour the hot broth around the outside.

Howard Street

ROAST WOOD PIGEON, CHARGRILLED MUSHROOM, CONFIT CELERY AND MUSHROOM VELOUTÉ

Serves 2

Core Ingredients

fillets of 1 pigeon crown
3 breakfast mushrooms
sourdough
2 celery sticks
100ml whole milk
20g cold butter
2 whole eggs
10g watercress
10g diced shallot
10g chopped chives
2 garlic cloves
2 sprigs thyme
50ml white wine
250ml good quality
    chicken stock
10ml white truffle oil

Method

1. Remove breasts from pigeon crown, check for any lead shot and set aside. **2.** Trim and peel breakfast mushrooms, set two aside. Keep trim along with the remaining mushroom. **3.** Trim and slightly peel celery, cut into 5cm long sticks. Keep trim for velouté. **4.** Cut sourdough into 1cm cubes, drizzle with olive oil and toast in pan until golden. **5.** Start velouté by adding half the diced shallot, celery trim, mushroom, mushroom trim and two garlic cloves to a pan with a splash of olive oil. Cook down for 10 minutes on a medium heat until lightly coloured. Set aside. **6.** Put celery sticks into small saucepan, cover with olive oil and gently cook with the sprigs of thyme until just tender. Remove and set aside. **7.** For the mushrooms, place mushrooms on a roasting tray, drizzle some olive oil, a couple of cubes of butter, rock salt and pepper and roast in an oven at 180°C for 10–12 minutes until tender and golden brown on the underside. Remove from tray and set aside.

Assembly

Heat a heavy-based frying pan and add oil. Season pigeon breasts with salt and pepper and gently fry in pan for 2–3 minutes on both sides for medium, 4–6 minutes for well done. Remove and place on kitchen roll, set aside in a warm place to rest. Heat a griddle pan until very hot and chargrill the mushrooms for 3 minutes. Return the mushroom velouté mix to the heat. In the pan add white wine and reduce until almost evaporated, add chicken stock and reduce by half. Whisk in milk and cold butter, season with salt and pepper, strain and keep warm. Crack eggs with egg topper, separate yolk from white and return yolk to the egg shell. Put shell into gently simmering water for 2–2½ minutes to warm through. Place the remaining diced shallot and a little rock salt on top of the yolk and fill the egg shell up with the mushroom velouté. On a warmed plate, assemble dish by first putting on mushroom with egg in the middle. Carve pigeon and allow one breast per person, place breast on plate. Place croutons around the mushroom and place celery sticks across the pigeon. Finally place watercress around the dish for presentation.

Howard Street

WHITE MOUSSE, DARK CHOCOLATE BROWNIE CRUMBLE, HONEYCOMB, POACHED STRAWBERRIES AND CRACKED BLACK PEPPER MERINGUE

Serves 2

Mousse

250g good quality white
 chocolate buttons
3 egg yolks
3 egg whites
100g caster sugar
250ml whipping cream
50ml white wine
5g leaf gelatine
10ml whipping cream

Brownie

75g dark chocolate buttons
75g diced butter
2 whole eggs
175g caster sugar
90g plain flour
40g chopped toasted hazelnuts
¼ tsp baking powder

Meringue

2 egg whites
125g caster sugar
10g cracked black pepper

Honeycomb

180g caster sugar
70g glucose
55g water
½ tsp bicarbonate of soda

Poached Strawberries

100g fresh strawberries
100g caster sugar
100ml balsamic vinegar
100ml port
50ml water
2 star anise

To Serve

20g fresh strawberries

Method

1. For the Mousse, put chocolate in bowl over simmering water. Heat until melted. **2.** In a mixer whip cream to soft peaks. Set aside. Whisk egg whites on high speed until meringue forms. Add 50g sugar to whites, one teaspoon at a time until glossy. Reduce speed to lowest. Soak gelatine in water for 5 minutes. **3.** Place large bowl over boiling water, add egg yolks, wine and 50g sugar. Whisk continuously until thick. Remove from heat. **4.** Boil 10ml whipping cream. Remove gelatine and squeeze out water. Add to cream and stir until dissolved. Fold melted chocolate into egg yolk mix, then fold in gelatine mix. **5.** Beat one-third meringue into egg/chocolate mix, then remainder. Fold in whipped cream. Refrigerate for 1 hour. **6.** For the Brownie, melt chocolate and butter in bowl over simmering water. Whip eggs and sugar on top speed until size doubled. Fold in melted chocolate mix, then flour and nuts. Line oven tray with greaseproof paper, pour in mixture, bake for 20–25 minutes at 170°C. **7.** For the Meringue, whisk egg whites on top speed until they firm up. Add sugar one teaspoon at a time until glossy. Fold in black pepper. Place greaseproof paper onto baking sheet and spread meringue evenly with spatula. Bake for 40 minutes at 100°C.

8. For the Honeycomb, heat sugar, glucose and water in pan until golden. Remove from heat and whisk in bicarbonate of soda. Pour onto pastry mat. **9.** For the Poached Strawberries, simmer sugar, balsamic vinegar, port, water and star anise in pan until sugar dissolved. Remove from heat, add halved strawberries and poach for 5 minutes.

Assembly

With a hot spoon scoop two spoons of mousse per person. Break up brownie and honeycomb and arrange around mousse. Add poached strawberries. Break meringue into shards and garnish with quartered strawberries.

Howard Street

JAMES ST. SOUTH

DAVID GILLMORE

JAMES ST. SOUTH: DAVID GILLMORE

Located in the very heart of Belfast city centre, James St. South opened in 2003 as an elegant statement of the arrival of groundbreaking Chef Niall McKenna. Housed in a historic linen mill, James St. South perfectly embodies the relationship between old and modern Belfast. It's both forward looking and innovative but firmly built on the best indigenous resources. Over the last decade, James St. South's interior and menu have been regularly and tastefully refreshed. However, its ethos of offering genuine hospitality while serving modern dishes using the best locally-sourced ingredients has remained the foundation for this highly respected restaurant.

Niall McKenna is recognised as one of the most innovative and demanding chefs in Belfast and has helped set the high standards of the contemporary restaurant scene in the city. His drive, talent and passion have been recognised with an array of hospitality awards and accolades including James St. South winning the Observer on Sunday Best Restaurant in Northern Ireland title three times. As Niall actively manages his other successful eateries clustered around the city, three years ago he handed the reins of his flagship restaurant to 35-year-old Chef David Gillmore. Originally from the Wirral in northwest England, David worked his way from catering college to a career in the kitchens of the prestigious five-star Chester Grosvenor Hotel, famous for maintaining its Michelin star since 1990.

After two years learning to prepare classic French cuisine to the highest standards in the kitchens of the Chester Grosvenor, David honed his naturally meticulous preparation and presentation skills. For him, the little things really matter. Attention to detail confirms to patrons he cares about their dining experience, and he wants them to feel looked after and ultimately satisfied. That satisfaction starts with the eyes and culminates in flavours in the mouth. This ostensibly simple ethos is what underpins all his dishes.

David draws inspiration from his early food memories of home-cooked, hearty, traditional meals made from the best local and seasonal produce. His modern interpretation of this honest approach to cooking is sophisticated dishes of pure theatre and sensory indulgence.

His training at another Michelin-starred restaurant, the famous Lords of the Manor Hotel located in the Cotswolds, introduced him to Heston Blumenthal-inspired 'molecular cooking' and enhanced his understanding and respect for attending to the smallest details in his dishes. He excels in combining flavours and textures to allow his ultra-fresh ingredients to shine independently and in concert. His food is complex without being complicated. It's down to earth with hidden depths, clean but moreish.

David's menu at James St. South is not about re-inventing the wheel; it's about making it run really smoothly.

He sticks to Niall McKenna's founding ethos of simple, elegant food made with the freshest local ingredients. Within those parameters, he has developed a personal style that openly embraces the natural food bounty of his adopted home. His dishes are intimate taste postcards evoking location and landscape. Starters include Chilled Portavogie Crab Lasagne; Lough Neagh Eel, Teryaki Mooli, Rosewater Cucumber and Miso; and King Scallops, Smoked Butter and Rathlin Island Kelp. The reverence for local produce continues with main courses that feature Antrim Fillet of Beef and Portavogie Langoustines – offered only in season of course.

David Gillmore creates memorable food that satisfies all the human senses, served in an ambiance of relaxed sophistication successfully fulfilling the long-standing expectations of James St. South's loyal patrons.

JAMES
ST.
SOUTH

POACHED WHITEHEAD LOBSTER, ORANGE, MEDJOOL DATE AND HELEN'S BAY LEAVES

Serves 4

Core Ingredients

1 × 500g lobster
2 oranges
4 peeled Medjool dates
selection of leaves
    (purslane, sorrel, watercress)
1 sheet feuille de brick
dulse

Orange Vinaigrette

2 oranges, zested
2 small oranges, juiced
30ml balsamic vinegar
40g honey
1 clove garlic, peeled
¾ tsp salt
¾ tsp freshly ground black pepper
175ml extra-virgin olive oil

Method

1. Blanch the lobster in boiling salted water for 5 minutes then refresh in iced water. Remove the lobster tail from the shell and remove the intestinal tract. Crack the claws and remove the shell, making sure you keep the claws whole. Remove the meat from the knuckles, chop roughly and keep to one side. **2.** Remove the skins from the dates and roll into small balls. **3.** Peel and slice one of the oranges. Depending on the season, blood oranges can be used as an alternative. **4.** Deep fry the dulse at 180°C until crisp. Brush the feuille de brick in rapeseed oil and season with sea salt. Bake in an oven at 200°C until golden brown. Allow to cool. **5.** For the Orange Vinaigrette, in a blender combine the orange zest, orange juice, balsamic vinegar, honey, garlic, salt and pepper. Blend until smooth. With the blender running, add the olive oil in a steady stream until combined.

Assembly

Brush the lobster tail and claw with vinaigrette and season with sea salt. Place a slice of orange onto the plate and set the lobster on it. Dress the leaves and neatly position. Garnish with the feuille de brick crisps and crispy dulse. To finish, grate fresh orange zest over the whole dish.

James St. South

COUNTY ANTRIM LAMB, NEW SEASON MORELS, SALSA VERDE AND WILD GARLIC

Serves 4

Core Ingredients
4 lamb rumps
16 cleaned fresh morels
wild garlic and flowers
purple sprouting broccoli
    and the leaves

Salsa Verde
handful of chopped flat
    parsley and wild garlic
1 tbsp capers
6 anchovy fillets
1 clove garlic
1 tbsp lemon juice
8 tbsp olive oil

Method
1. Prepare the lamb loin by removing all sinew. Place in a hot pan and colour on all sides. Place in oven set at 180°C and cook to medium rare. Allow to rest for 5 minutes. **2.** Mix the chopped parsley and wild garlic. Add chopped capers, anchovies, crushed garlic and lemon juice. Gradually beat in the olive oil and set aside. **3.** Blanch the purple broccoli along with the leaves in boiling salted water. **4.** To cook the morels, fry in a small amount of oil in a hot pan, add a knob of butter and season well with salt and pepper.

Assembly
To serve, dress the plate in salsa verde. Carve the rested lamb and season with sea salt. Garnish with the cooked morels, wilted wild garlic leaf, purple broccoli and wild garlic flowers. Serve with a jug of lamb jus.

SMOKED CHOCOLATE, LIME SORBET, TOASTED MERINGUE AND PISTACHIO NUTS

Serves 4

Core Ingredients
500ml whipping cream
25g butter
500g smoked dark chocolate
2½ limes, zested
5 limes, juiced

Lime Sorbet
250ml lime juice
250ml milk
250ml water
250g sugar

Chocolate Crumb
280g butter
180g caster sugar
100g egg whites
400g cocoa powder

Italian Meringue
100g egg whites
200g sugar
water

Garnish
pistachio nuts
smoked chocolate, grated

Method
1. Heat cream and lime. Pour over chocolate and add butter. Pour into a container and allow to set in the refrigerator. **2.** For the Lime Sorbet, bring lime juice, milk, water and sugar to the boil. Pass through a fine sieve. Allow to cool and then churn in an ice cream machine. **3.** For the Chocolate Crumb, beat butter and sugar together. Mix whites and cocoa powder together and mix with butter and sugar. Cook at 180°C until like a biscuit, then crush into small pieces. **4.** For the Italian Meringue, heat sugar and water to 118°C and pour on to whisking egg whites. Whisk until cool. Place in piping bag until required.

Assembly
Place a quenelle of the smoked chocolate into the grated chocolate and coat. Put onto the plate and top with the meringue. Blow torch the meringue until golden. Position the pistachio nuts in the meringue and serve the lime sorbet alongside.

MOURNE SEAFOOD BAR

ANDY REA

MOURNE SEAFOOD BAR: ANDY REA

Since opening in 2006, Mourne Seafood Bar, located on historic Bank Square, has become an institution in the Belfast food scene. It's a firm favourite with locals and tourists alike with its honest, authentic, no-nonsense approach. The menu is a continual celebration of locally-caught fish and seafood, delivered daily and prepared with a lightness of touch that requires understated confidence and skill.

In his youth, Belfast-born Chef Andy Rea perfected his impressive skills and expertise with seafood in the kitchens of some of the best restaurants in Martha's Vineyard and Cape Cod. He returned to Belfast in the mid-1990s to head up Paul Rankin's landmark restaurants Roscoff and then Cayenne. Building on a foundation of excellence, he became one of the second wave of innovative chefs to have a significant influence on the city's food scene.

Since the inception of Mourne Seafood Bar, Andy has developed a confident but rustic cooking style. His ethos is the less you do to fresh local fish, the better it tastes. So in Mourne Seafood Bar, he serves seasonal fish cooked to perfection with heads and tails on, heaps of steaming mussels in pots, raw meaty oysters and succulent crab claws in their shells. With his down-to-earth approach, Andy believes a big part of the enjoyment of seafood is the effort you have to put in to get the best bits out. It's a primal experience he wholeheartedly encourages.

In the middle of a bustling city, Mourne Seafood Bar magically evokes comforting childhood memories of holidays by the sea and long summer days lit by golden sunlight.

Andy describes his relaxed cooking style as 'unplugged', inventively creating menu specials from whatever ingredients local suppliers bring fresh to his door every morning. This daily challenge stimulates culinary creativity in his kitchen and introduces diners to a constantly shifting kaleidoscope of new flavours. Due to patron demand, some of Andy's most beloved dishes have been on the menu for a decade. The sublime Salt and Chilli Squid with Napa Slaw, Chilli Jam and Mayo, or the ever-popular Mourne Mussels with White Wine, Garlic and Cream, provide a familiar framework for his exciting daily specials. That dynamic combination keeps diners enthusiastically coming back for more. In Mourne Seafood Bar booking is essential as tables are always in high demand.

Like his restaurant, Andy Rea is firmly grounded in the locality. Mourne Seafood Bar is built on Belfast's historical foundations; during fit out for the opening, oyster shells from the 19th century were found in abundance in its exposed foundations. This unearthed evidence indicates the important role seafood once played for ordinary city residents as a cheap source of nutrition. It's appropriate then that Mourne Seafood Bar is situated in an area where historically the local catch was essential to the community.

Andy's mission has always been to make Belfast fall in love with fish again by offering simple but stunning fresh produce at an affordable price in a welcoming city venue.

The history of Mourne Seafood Bar is solid and its future is bright. Andy has invested time and effort into nurturing the careers of young, talented staff, acting as a supportive teacher and mentor. The restaurant's Manager Sean Fitzpatrick and Head Chef Niall Sarhan have both worked for Andy since they left school 16 years ago. Now they are key contributors to the evolution and future development of Mourne Seafood Bar. After 28 years in the upper echelons of the hospitality industry, Andy Rea is renowned for his innovation, energy and generosity of spirit. He appreciates and utilises local resources to their maximum potential, producing exciting, authentic food in a restaurant with real personality. He is both an inspiration and ambassador for the best the city has to offer and has consistently championed local artisan producers and suppliers. His early belief, pride and investment in his home city have helped establish a local food supply network and chef fraternity that are the very foundations for the flourishing food scene Belfast now enjoys.

who picked up a yawning
finger caught in the snapped shut shell.
The conclusion was predictable. When the man
freed his finger and put it into his mouth to
relieve the pain, he tasted the oyster liquor
and discovered that the incredible oyster was
also edible.

RAZOR CLAM FRITTERS
WITH SAFFRON AIOLI AND RED PEPPER SALSA

Serves 4

Core Ingredients

1 cup plain flour
1 tsp baking powder
¼ tsp sea salt
1 pinch cayenne pepper
1 egg
3 tbsp lager, approximately
175g razor clams, minced
    (remove black stomach
    before mincing)
1 tbsp tarragon, chopped
1 tbsp chives, chopped
1 pinch cumin

Saffron Aioli

1 tbsp Dijon mustard
6 strands saffron infused
    in 2 tbsp boiling water
½ lemon, juiced
1 clove garlic, minced
sea salt and cracked
    black pepper
150ml vegetable oil

Red Pepper Salsa

10g basil leaves, shredded
2 plum tomatoes, diced
    (no seeds)
2 roasted red peppers, diced
1 tsp chives, chopped
sea salt and cracked
    black pepper
2 tbsp rice vinegar
1 tbsp sugar
2 tbsp ketchup
1 tsp smoked Tabasco

Method

1. In a bowl, combine all dry core ingredients, then mix together with wet ingredients to make a batter – don't overwork. **2.** In a fryer, heat oil to 180°C, spoon batter mix carefully into fryer, fry until pale brown. Remove and rest for at least 4 minutes before frying until golden. **3.** Remove from fryer onto kitchen towel, lightly season with sea salt and cayenne pepper. **4.** For the Saffron Aioli, add all ingredients, except the oil, into a bowl, slowly add in oil while whisking with an electric hand mixer or blender. When aioli is thick adjust seasoning. **5.** For the Red Pepper Salsa, mix all ingredients together and adjust seasoning.

Assembly

Plate up fritters, aioli and salsa as soon as it's ready.

Mourne Seafood Bar

ROAST FILLET OF HAKE WITH SALT COD SKORDALIA, SAVOY CABBAGE AND BACON GREMOLATA

Serves 4

Core Ingredients
4 × 180g fillets of hake

Skordalia
250g potatoes, peeled and sliced
150g salt cod (soak cod for
    24 hours, changing water
    every 6 hours)
150ml light olive oil
4 cloves garlic, crushed
1 bay leaf
1 sprig rosemary
4 tbsp milk, approximately

Bacon Gremolata
8 rashers smoked streaky
    bacon or pancetta
½ bunch parsley, chopped
zest 1 lemon

Savoy Cabbage
½ savoy cabbage,
    finely shredded
bacon fat (reserved from
    Bacon Gremolata)

Method
1. Preheat oven to 180°C. **2.** Cut cod into small pieces, place in a casserole dish with olive oil, potatoes, garlic, bay leaf and rosemary. Wrap tight with tin foil and bake for approximately 1 hour until potatoes are soft. **3.** Retain half of the oil from the casserole dish. Empty the rest of the contents of the casserole dish into a food processor and blend until smooth then add milk. Adjust consistency with milk and more oil. **4.** Cook bacon until crispy and retain bacon fat from cooking.
5. Once cool, chop bacon fine and mix with parsley and lemon.
6. Boil cabbage in seasoned water until cooked. **7.** Remove cabbage, strain and set aside. Reheat cabbage in bacon fat from cooking the rashers previously.

Assembly
Place a large non-stick pan over a high heat, season fish on both sides. Add a drizzle of oil to pan and a small knob of butter. When butter starts to brown, quickly add fish skin side down. Once skin is golden and crispy, turn fish and place in a hot oven for 6 minutes then serve with skordalia, cabbage and gremolata, as shown.

Mourne Seafood Bar

SMOKED SALMON WITH SESAME CRUSTED SUSHI RICE, SEAWEED SALAD AND PONZU DRESSING

Serves 4

Core Ingredients

400g smoked salmon, sliced
10g dried wakame seaweed,
    rehydrate in boiling water
    for 1 minute
10g Japanese pickled ginger
25g white radish,
    cut into fine strips
25g red radish, sliced
50g cucumber, cut into
    fine strips (no seeds)

Sushi Rice

1 cup sushi rice
1 tsp sea salt
3 tsp sugar
3 tbsp Japanese rice vinegar
2 tbsp toasted black and white
    sesame seeds

Ponzu Dressing

¼ cup Kikkoman soy sauce
    (reduced salt)
2 tbsp lemon juice
1 tbsp mirin
pinch crushed red peppers
2 tbsp lime juice

Method

1. Place rice into a bowl, gently run under cold water until water runs clear for approximately 3 minutes, then drain. **2.** Place one cup of water and drained rice into a small saucepan. Place over high heat. Bring to the boil uncovered. Once it begins to boil, reduce the heat to the lowest setting and cover. Cook for approximately 15 minutes. Remove from the heat and let stand, covered, for 10 minutes.
3. Combine the rice vinegar, sugar and salt in a small bowl and heat in the microwave on a high heat for 30 seconds. In a large bowl, add rice and ½ rice vinegar mix. Combine and allow to cool.
4. Mound sushi rice into four small cakes, roll in sesame seeds to finish. **5.** Dress radish and cucumber with remaining rice vinegar mix. **6.** For the Ponzu Dressing, mix all of the ingredients together.

Assembly

Arrange smoked salmon on a plate. Top smoked salmon with wakame seaweed and pickled ginger. Place rice cake in the centre and top with cucumber and radish salad. Sprinkle with crushed peppers (optional) and dress salmon with Ponzu dressing.

NEILL'S HILL

CATH GRADWELL AND JONATHAN DAVIS

NEILL'S HILL: CATH GRADWELL AND JONATHAN DAVIS

Neill's Hill, located at Ballyhackamore in East Belfast, is named after a long-forgotten railway station decommissioned in 1950 and consumed by the city's advancing urban sprawl. It's owned and run by 49-year-old Jonathan Davis, universally recognised as restaurant royalty in Belfast as the son of the man who opened one of the city's first and most beloved eateries, Skandia, in 1967. His dynastic heritage means he has hospitality in his DNA, and he instinctively knows how the restaurant trade works. Jonathan studied Hotel Management at the University of Ulster and spent a year's placement at the Tara Hotel in London. His youthful summers were also occupied working both front of house and in the kitchen of Skandia. So when the time came to open his own restaurant, he had high expectations and demanding standards. He admits that he never harboured any ambition to be a chef, knowing how difficult a job it actually is, instead focusing on developing 360-degree vision of how great restaurants operate and consistently deliver.

Fifty-one-year-old Cath is a 'blow in' who grew up in Bolton in the North of England. At 21, she trained under the demanding tutelage of the godfathers of modern restaurant cuisine, the Roux brothers, at their city restaurant Le Poulbot in London, before moving with its Head Chef Rowley Leigh for the opening of the revolutionary restaurant Kensington Place. A year in this intense environment instilled a work ethos in Cath that remains with her to this day.

She moved to Belfast to work with celebrity Chef Paul Rankin in his groundbreaking restaurant Roscoff in the early 1990s and quickly made the city her home. By the middle of that decade, Jonathan was also making plans to open his first restaurant, Alden's. In a pioneering, if somewhat risky move, he located his new fine dining eatery at Ballyhackmore in East Belfast, a little outside the city's traditional food districts. To attract the epicurious, he was aware that he needed a brilliant chef in the kitchen and Cath amply fulfilled that demanding brief. When the acclaimed Alden's opened in 1997, it quickly gained a reputation for exceptional food and a wine list unrivalled in the city. It was a huge success, despite often-difficult trading conditions – a testament to the quality of food on offer and the unique ambience created by Jonathan's vision. So it came as a surprise to many when he unexpectedly rolled down the shutters in 2012, stripped out the trappings of fine dining and launched his new restaurant space as the modern, neighbourhood bistro Neill's Hill. Lacking emotional sentimentality, the seasoned restaurateur knew it was time for change to match market demands and his new bistro emerged as the antithesis to its formal predecessor. Its new incarnation has an on-trend, homemade authenticity to it.

During the transition period, Cath dedicated her time to teaching young chefs at Belfast Metropolitan College, an experience she credits with making her a better and more relaxed chef. It provided a career hiatus affording her time to reflect and mature her personal cooking style. Opening Neill's Hill, Jonathan knew he needed the essential ingredient for success – Chef Cath Gradwell. Had anyone but Jonathan asked her to step back into the intense environment of a busy professional kitchen, she would have politely declined. But there is an easy-going, sibling-like relationship between the two fostered over many years working together. That well-established bond of trust means their combined talents and decades of experience bring a confidence and stability that attracts patrons in their droves. The modern menu is democratically priced and easily accessible: Aged Irish Sirloin served with a choice of Garlic Butter, Blue Cheese or Pepper Sauce remains a perennial favourite, while sharing jars of Potted Shrimp served with Hot Toast or Hummus with Grilled Flatbread encourage conversation and conviviality.

After so many years in the business, Jonathan and Cath remain open, pragmatic and passionate about food, wine and hospitality. They are both gastronomic pioneers who have consistently set high standards. They have quietly punched in the hours and ploughed in the effort for decades, contributing to raising the city's culinary standards. They both deserve the highest credit for helping put Belfast firmly on the international culinary map.

SIZZLING PORTAVOGIE PRAWNS WITH CHORIZO, GARLIC AND CHILLI

Serves 2

Core Ingredients
60ml olive oil
15g chorizo, diced
8 thin rounds red chilli
    with seeds
8 thin slices garlic
    (dried for more impact)
pinch smoked paprika
60g Portavogie prawns

To Serve
pinch salt
¼ small lemon, juiced
2 tsp flat parsley
shredded bread

Method
1. Heat iron skillet in oven at 200°C.
2. Add ingredients to skillet and sizzle for two minutes. **3.** If you don't have a skillet, heat ingredients in a small pan until the prawns lose the translucent appearance.

Assembly
Season with salt and lemon juice. Serve with flat parsley and bread.

Neill's Hill

ROAST FILLET OF HAKE WITH TOMATO, WHITE BEAN AND CHORIZO STEW

Serves 4

Core Ingredients
4 hake fillets

Chorizo Stew
2 tbsp vegetable oil
1 small onion, peeled
    and finely diced
2 cloves garlic, finely grated
40g sliced chorizo
2 tsp tomato purée
1 × 400g tin chopped tomatoes
1 tbsp tomato ketchup
1 × 400g tin cannellini beans
    or mixed beans
2 pinches oregano
1 tbsp flat parsley, shredded
1 tbsp coriander, shredded
salt
pepper

To Serve
green vegetables (samphire)
green salad

Method
1. For the Chorizo Stew, warm the vegetable oil in a small pot and add the onion. Cook gently without colour until soft, stirring occasionally. Add the garlic, chorizo and tomato purée and cook gently for a further 5 minutes, stirring occasionally. 2. Add chopped tomatoes and tomato ketchup and simmer for 5 minutes so it thickens slightly. 3. Add the well drained beans, oregano, parsley and coriander and gently bring to the boil, simmer for 5 minutes. Adjust by adding water if too thick or continue to simmer if too saucy. 4. Taste and season with salt and pepper, if required. The stew can be made in advance and refrigerated for up to a week. 5. To cook the hake, preheat oven to 200°C. On the hob warm two tablespoons of vegetable oil. 6. Season the hake all over with salt, place skin side down in the oil and fry gently until the skin starts to brown. 7. Transfer the pan to the hot oven and roast the hake for 10–12 minutes depending on the thickness of the fish.

Assembly
Heat the bean stew in a pan and divide between four bowls. Using a fish slice, place a portion of hake skin side up on top of each stew. Serve with a buttered green vegetable of your choice (for example, samphire) or a crisp green salad.

Neill's Hill

ROAST CÔTE DE BOEUF WITH CHIMICHURRI

Serves 2

Core Ingredients
900g côte de boeuf (large rib
    steak on the bone)
vegetable oil
salt
pepper

Chimichurri Sauce
50g flat parsley
1 ¼ tsp dried oregano
3 cloves garlic, peeled
¼ onion, peeled
1 tsp chilli flakes
6 tbsp olive oil
½ lemon, juiced
3 tsp red wine vinegar
25g fresh coriander

To Serve
rocket and Parmesan salad

Method
1. Preheat the oven to maximum.
Bring the meat to room temperature
and season well all over with salt
and pepper. In an overproof pan on
the hob, brown the meat all over in
a little vegetable oil. 2. Place in oven
for approximately 7 minutes and
then turn the meat over. Return to
oven for another 7 minutes. Note:
these timings are based on cooking
medium rare using a furnace-like
industrial oven – the timing should
be adjusted to suit domestic oven
and preferred cooking requirements.
3. Remove from oven and loosely
cover with foil to keep warm.
Allow to rest for 10–12 minutes.
4. For the Chimichurri Sauce,
blitz all ingredients in a liquidiser
leaving a little bit of texture.
Alternatively, finely chop
everything by hand and mix.

Assembly
Slice the beef and serve on a
platter with rocket and Parmesan
salad and a dish of chimichurri.
Let everyone help themselves.

Neill's Hill

OX

STEPHEN TOMAN

OX: STEPHEN TOMAN

In 2013 a food revolution, not seen in Belfast since 1984 when Chef Paul Rankin opened Roscoff, began quietly fermenting when young Chef Stephen Toman along with close friend Alain Kerloc'h opened OX. With an impressive high ceiling, intimate mezzanine level, industrial lighting, salvaged furniture and a utilitarian open kitchen, on a shoestring budget a 32-year-old Stephen transformed a former tile shop into one of the most exciting restaurants in Ireland. The whitewashed brick walls of OX are intentionally devoid of artistic adornment because the real art is on diners' plates. In just three years, his singular vision, inventiveness and the uncompromising quality of his food has attracted a clutch of prestigious awards including: The Good Food Guide 2016 Editors' Awards – Restaurant of the Year, Catey Awards 2015 – Menu of the Year United Kingdom, World's 50 Best Restaurants 2015 – Hottest Restaurant to Visit in Western Europe, Food & Wine Magazine – Chef of the Year and Restaurant of the Year and many, many more. It's hard to believe it all started with a teenage Stephen working in a chip shop in West Belfast.

Food is the main passion of Stephen's life. Aged 16, he was offered work experience in Planks restaurant on the Lisburn Road, cementing his passion for working in a busy professional kitchen and starting him on a career and life journey culminating in the opening of OX.

After three years diligently working his way up to the position of Sous Chef, Stephen wanted to learn how to cater for large numbers and took a job at Dukes Hotel in Belfast. Working under a characterful French Head Chef, he got his first taste of classic cuisine. But more significantly, the romantic tales of foodie adventures spun by his mentor beguiled him. Seduced by visions of gastronomic Paris, at 19 he vowed he would work in a three-Michelin-star restaurant in the world capital of cuisine. He then spent a year working in Ten Square's Porcelain before travelling to Arizona where he spent a year in a five-star hotel, thriving on the pace and camaraderie of a big professional team dedicated to quality.

In 2003 Stephen went to work at the newly-opened James St. South. Knowing in his heart he too would one day open his own restaurant in the city, it provided the perfect insight into the hard work required. But after a few years, Stephen was still dreaming about life as a chef in Paris. Still young enough to not fear the consequences, he impulsively decided to move there – despite having no plan, no money, and no French language skills. In 2005, living in a small bedsit, he bought the Parisian Michelin guide and tramped the streets of the city rapping on every three-star kitchen back door asking for a job. Surviving on pennies, living in the gutter, he was still looking at the stars – Michelin stars.

His perseverance paid off and he secured a position at Le Taillevent and also staged at L' Astrance, Robuchon and L'arpege owned by Alain Passard – recognised as one of the world's greatest chefs.

Back in Belfast in 2006, he returned to James St. South and over the next two years worked his way up to the position of Head Chef, refining his own unique personal cooking style, obsessively reading cookbooks and continuing staging in Paris' finest restaurants. Stephen believes attitude dictates altitude and his dedication drove him to open his own high-flying restaurant. He is so brilliant at what he does, quietly redefining modern Irish cuisine, it was almost inevitable a Michelin star would shine on him. In 2015, he achieved his lifelong goal when OX was awarded that most revered honour after just two years of opening. Stephen is a genuine visionary food pioneer who has already changed the face of the Belfast restaurant scene through the persuasiveness of his cooking. His dishes are a poetic combination of chaos and symmetry built on a foundation of the best seasonal produce. Talent hits a target no one else can hit; genius hits a target no one else can see.

CAULIFLOWER, VEAL SWEETBREADS, PARMESAN, HAZELNUT, BURNT ONION

Serves 2

Core Ingredients
100g veal sweetbreads
25g butter
1 small cauliflower
1 tbsp hazelnuts,
    peeled and chopped

Burnt Onion Powder
500g onions, thinly sliced

Parmesan Royale
125g Parmesan
75g cream
2 whole eggs
1 egg yolk

Method
1. Begin by preparing the sweetbreads a day in advance. Soak in a container of iced water, change the water at least twice. After 24 hours, remove the sweetbreads from the water and use a sharp knife to remove any sinew. **2.** For the Burnt Onion Powder, place the sliced onions onto an oven tray lined with greaseproof paper and set into a hot oven (180–200°C), roast until blackened, then lower the temperature to 100°C for 1 hour. Remove the burnt onions from the oven and allow to cool, then place into a food processor and blitz to a fine powder. **3.** For the Parmesan Royale, add Parmesan, cream and eggs to a Thermomix® and set at 70°C for 7 minutes at number five. Remove and cool. **4.** Use a mandolin to shave the cauliflower finely and place in iced water. Just before serving, remove from the water, season and lightly grill until tender. **5.** Roast the hazelnuts, place in a clean tea towel and rub vigorously to remove the skin. **6.** Season and cook the sweetbreads in a hot pan with butter for 4 minutes on either side until caramelised and firm to touch, continuously baste with butter during cooking. Rest in a warm place.

Assembly
Carve the sweetbreads and arrange onto warm plates, sprinkle with hazelnuts and garnish with grilled cauliflower, spoon a little Parmesan Royale onto the plate and dust with onion powder.

OX

ASPARAGUS, YOLK, NETTLES, OYSTER MUSHROOM

Serves 2

Core Ingredients
4 English green asparagus spears
8 wild asparagus spears
nasturtium leaves
chive flower

Nettle Purée
1 cup wild nettles
½ cup baby spinach

Mushroom
2 small oyster mushrooms
20g butter
fleur de sel
pepper

Egg Yolk
4 whole eggs
    (to allow for breakages)

Method
1. For the Nettle Purée, pick and wash the nettles and baby spinach and then blanch in boiling water for 1 minute and refresh in iced water. Purée until smooth (add a little water if necessary), season and pass through a fine sieve. **2.** For the Mushroom, peel the oyster mushrooms, gently cook in a non-stick pan until golden with butter and seasoning. **3.** For the Egg Yolk, emerge the whole eggs in a water bath (65°C) and cook for 35 minutes.

Assembly
Peel asparagus and blanch in boiling water for 1½ minutes until 'al dente' and arrange on a plate. Meanwhile heat the nettle purée and spoon onto the plate. Peel the hot egg, carefully remove the yolk and place beside the purée. Garnish with oyster mushroom, nasturtium leaves, chive flower petals and sprinkle with fleur de sel.

OX

CARAMELISED PINEAPPLE, STAR ANISE, SABLÉ

Serves 4

Sablé (makes 290g)
90g butter
60g sugar
25g egg yolk
120g flour, sieved

**Star Anise
Crème Pâtissière**
125ml milk
2 star anise
50g egg yolk
35g caster sugar
5g cornflour
5g plain flour

Caramelised Pineapple
2 tbsp caster sugar
4 wedges fresh pineapple
    (small enough to fit inside
    the sugar cylinder)
4 star anise
1 tbsp glucose

Sugar Cylinder
200g caster sugar
1 tbsp glucose
1 tbsp water

Method

1. For the Sablé, cream butter and sugar together, gradually add egg yolks, flour and mix to smooth paste. Wrap paste in cling film and refrigerate for 45 minutes before rolling into thin sheets, cut into rectangles (to fit inside the sugar cylinder), transfer to a baking sheet and bake at 160°C until golden and crisp. **2.** For the Star Anise Crème Pâtissière, boil milk and star anise in a saucepan, remove from heat to infuse for 30 minutes. Pass through a fine sieve and remove star anise. Return saucepan of milk to the heat. Whisk egg yolks, sugar, cornflour and flour in a large mixing bowl, add hot milk and whisk to a smooth consistency, return all to saucepan, bring back to the boil and whisk for 2–3 minutes until thick. Spoon into a bowl and cover with cling film to prevent a skin forming while cooling. **3.** For the Caramelised Pineapple, place half of the sugar into a vacuum bag with pineapple wedges and star anise and cook in a bain marie (85°C) for 1 hour until tender. Just before assembly, sprinkle the remaining tablespoon of sugar into a frying pan and cook to a light caramel, add pineapple wedges, star anise and caramelise.
4. For the Sugar Cylinder, add sugar to a saucepan with glucose and water, cook to a golden caramel and then pour onto a silicone mat to cool completely. Break the caramel into a food processor and blitz to a fine powder.

5. Make four rectangles of powder on a baking tray lined with silicone and place in a low oven (110°C) to melt. When slightly cool, lift using a palette knife and wrap around a small plastic rolling pin to make four cylinders. Leave to cool.

Assembly
Spoon crème pâtissière onto the plate. Place caramelised pineapple onto the sablé and carefully push inside the sugar cylinder. Place the cylinder on top of the crème pâtissière and serve with saffron or vanilla ice cream.

OX

SAPHYRE

PATRICK ROWAN

SAPHYRE: PATRICK ROWAN

Saphyre, located at the start of the Lisburn Road, is one of the city's newest and finest restaurants. Secreted at the back of a former gothic-style church where acclaimed local interior designer Kris Turnbull has his showroom, it is a wonderland fantasy of style and taste where the interior and menu are thoughtfully coordinated. Opened in 2013, Saphyre is a hidden gem where Kris has created his own little world dedicated to the highest standards of hospitality and fine dining. From the gold leaf covered wall sconces to the understated colour scheme of emerald green, inky blue and ochre, inspired by a gloriously detailed painting of the feathers of an exotic bird's wing by German Renaissance artist Albrecht Durer, Saphyre is truly a bijoux masterpiece. The atmosphere is relaxed and unstuffy, and this well-considered restaurant is the perfect warm and welcoming stage for young Chef Patrick Rowan to present his fantastically magical food.

Aged just 31, Patrick is as considered and thoughtful as the restaurant itself. A decade ago, he felt his life was lacking in direction when his adolescent fantasy of becoming a professional footballer proved elusive. But living in Donaghadee afforded him an opportunity right on his doorstep that would change the direction of his life and quickly put him at the top of the culinary premiership. At 21, he took a job in the kitchen of one of Northern Ireland's top gastro pubs, Pier 36, where his introduction into the world of the professional kitchen was an encouraging one. He was taken under the wing of the pub's head chef who taught him a wide range of basic culinary skills and the joys of presenting locally-caught seafood. After two years at Pier 36, he forsook the gentle backwaters of County Down to enter the high-octane world of pioneering Chef Paul Rankin at his acclaimed Cayenne in Belfast. It was at this world-class restaurant Patrick was introduced to sophisticated flavours and fine dining presentation. But after a stint at The Boathouse in Bangor learning to prepare modern, funky cuisine, he accelerated his career by securing a position at Michelin-starred Chef Jason Atherton's acclaimed restaurant Pollen Street Social, located on London's exclusive Mayfair. He enjoyed being pushed to the limits on a daily basis as every dish leaving the kitchen demanded perfection. That attention to detail is evident in both the presentation and flavours of the dishes on his inspiring Saphyre menu today.

In 2012, Patrick returned to Northern Ireland to work under award-winning talented Chef Danny Millar at his destination restaurant Balloo House in Killinchy, famous for a menu full of indigenous ingredients. Patrick absorbed Danny's experience and knowledge like a sponge and thrived on the high expectations of the menu. His commitment and talent were noted, and he quickly became Senior Sous Chef and Acting Head Chef working closely with Danny to create exceptional menus founded on the very best fresh local ingredients. Patrick aspired to emulate his chef heroes and throughout his career has strategically placed himself to learn from the best in the business. In 2014, he effectively auditioned for the position of Head Chef in Saphyre, and in just two years, due to the combined talents of owner/designer Kris and Chef Patrick, Saphyre is now presenting some of the most exciting food in the city. The menu, which reflects seasonality, is whimsical and evocative and presented with exacting precision for visual impact, underpinned by innovative flavour and texture combinations. The À La Carte menu features dishes like Kilkeel Crab served with White Asparagus and Nashi Pear or Cod with Nasturtium and Broad Beans presented in Mushroom Broth.

There is an emotional resonance underpinning Patrick's food. In his kitchen, he consciously conjures an enticing air of mystery to stimulate diners' curiosity before they even have an opportunity to taste. Despite his youth, he is a naturally intuitive chef who knows how to heighten expectations and build anticipation, thus enhancing the overall dining experience. To achieve this level of excellence consistently is difficult but Patrick has risen to the challenge with aplomb. Saphyre is quietly pushing the boundaries of food in the city with its constantly changing, bespoke taster menus of glamorous culinary theatre and its deliciously exciting daily menu presentations designed to delight its already devoted patrons.

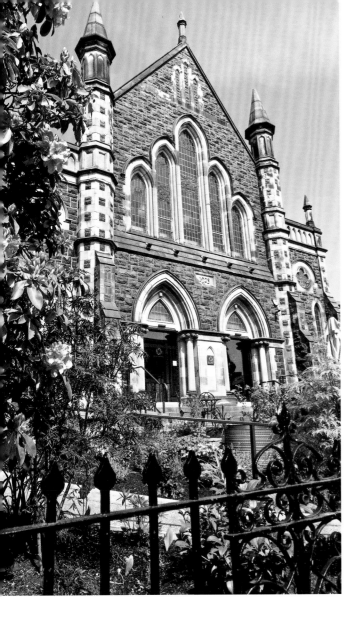

LANGOUSTINES, RHUBARB, GINGER AND YOGURT

Serves 4

Core Ingredients
langoustines
lemon juice
sea salt

Clandeboye Estate Yoghurt Espuma
12 large fresh langoustine
    tails, raw and peeled
450g Clandeboye Estate
    Greek yogurt
1 gelatine leaf
100g whipping cream

Poached Rhubarb
2 forced rhubarb stalks
50g grenadine
2 star anise
10 pink peppercorns
2cm fresh ginger,
    thinly sliced

Pickled Ginger Gel
100g liquid reserved
    from one packet
    of pickled ginger
1g ultratex

To Serve
watercress

Method
1. For the Clandeboye Estate Yogurt Espuma, soak the gelatine leaf in cold water for 2 minutes. Heat the cream up to just below boiling and dissolve the gelatine through the cream. Fold the cream through the yogurt and transfer to a ½ litre whipper gun. Charge the gun twice with nitrous oxide charges. 2. For the Poached Rhubarb, cut four 10cm slices of rhubarb and place in a vacuum pouch. Combine the grenadine, star anise, pink peppercorns and fresh ginger and bring to the boil. Allow the mixture to cool down and infuse. Once cool, add to the rhubarb and seal the bag hard. Cook in a water bath at 62.5°C for approximately 15 minutes until just tender. Alternatively, the rhubarb can be poached in a pot not letting the temperature exceed 70°C for around 5 minutes. 3. For the Pickled Ginger Gel, whisk the ultratex into the reserved pickled ginger juice and leave to set for 5 minutes. Add a little more ultratex if the gel has not got the right viscosity. 4. Season the langoustines with sea salt and, using a blow torch, scorch each tail until it starts to blacken. Squeeze fresh lemon juice over the tails.

Assembly
Place the cooked rhubarb in the centre of a plate and arrange three langoustines around it. Place little dots of the pickled ginger gel around the plate and garnish with three pieces of picked watercress. Finally, pipe the yogurt espuma onto the centre of the plate, serve immediately.

Saphyre

ROAST COD, MUSHROOM BROTH, BROAD BEANS AND NASTURTIUMS

Serves 4

Core Ingredients
1 side cod, pin bones
    and skin removed
50g broad beans, shelled
8 button mushrooms,
    thinly sliced lengthways
    through a mandolin
12 broad bean flowers
flaked sea salt
lemon juice

Mushroom Broth
500g brown chicken stock
500g roast fish stock
30g dried porcini mushrooms
salt

Method
1. Preheat oven to 180°C. **2.** For
the Mushroom Broth, combine
the chicken stock, fish stock, dried
porcini mushrooms and reduce
by half. Add salt to required taste.
Pass through a sieve and keep warm.
3. Using a sharp knife remove the
loin from the side of the cod and
portion it into four. **4.** Sear the cod
top side up in a non-stick frying pan
until golden brown and place in
the oven for 4 minutes until just
cooked through. Remove from the
pan, season with flaked sea salt and
lemon juice. **5.** In a pot of salted
water, cook the broad beans for
approximately 1 minute until there
is just a little bite in them.

Assembly
Place the cooked cod loin in a
bowl and garnish with the broad
beans, button mushrooms,
nasturtiums and broad bean
flowers. Pour broth tableside.

Saphyre

APPLE PARFAIT, SWEET CIDER CONSOMMÉ AND GRANOLA

Serves 8

Apple Parfait

30g water
100g caster sugar
6 egg yolks
300g apple purée
25g pomme verte
250g double cream,
   whipped to soft peaks
20g lemon juice
100g granola

Green Apple Glaze

16½g gold leaf gelatine
210g apple purée
105g caster sugar
210g glucose
140g double cream
210g white chocolate
5g green food colouring

Sweet Cider Consommé

750g Long Meadow sweet cider
50g honey
50g sugar
20g lemon juice

Method

1. For the Apple Parfait, mix the water and sugar and boil to 120°C. Whisk the egg yolks in a stand up mixer until pale and slowly add the sugar syrup. Whisk until the mixture is cold. **2.** Combine the apple purée and pomme verte and fold in the whipped cream. Fold in the egg sabayon and finish with lemon juice. **3.** Pour the parfait mix into demi-sphere moulds and freeze until required. **4.** For the Green Apple Glaze, soak gelatine in cold water. Place the apple purée, caster sugar, green food colouring and glucose in a saucepan and boil to 103°C. Remove the pot from the heat and dissolve the gelatine in the mixture. **5.** Add the cream and then pour the mixture over the white chocolate and emulsify with a stick blender. Allow the mixture to cool to between 35 and 40°C. **6.** Once cool, pour the glaze over the de-moulded apple parfait and place in the freezer until presentation. **7.** For the Sweet Cider Consommé, reduce 500g of the cider by half. Add the remaining ingredients and bring back to the boil. Add the lemon juice and pass the liquid through a sieve lined with muslin cloth, allowing it to drip through slowly.

Assembly

Remove the glazed parfait from the freezer and gently press the granola around the base. Place the parfait in the bowl and pour the consommé tableside.

Saphyre

SHU

BRIAN McCANN

SHU: BRIAN McCANN

Chef Brian McCann is a self-confessed obsessive. The 38-year-old constantly fizzes with enthusiasm for life and his craft. Those personal qualities have made him one of the most celebrated and respected chefs in Belfast today. He is a man of passion and he unselfconsciously immerses himself into whatever he is doing. It's that level of commitment that makes him so good at what he does. He grew up in West Belfast, just a few miles from where he now holds court as Head Chef in one of the city's perennially popular eateries, Shu. But his journey to lead this famed and celebrated kitchen has taken 23 years and a culinary trip around the world.

Brian started his career in catering by default after realising formal education was insufficient to contain his youthful energy and curiosity. As a teenager, his first job was at the Balmoral Hotel in South Belfast. He was attracted like a moth to the flame by the buzz and energy of the kitchen. At a formative age, it also afforded him good pocket money and a degree of independence – something Brian clearly thrives on. His career journey began in earnest when he left Belfast for the kitchens of London in 1998. There he had spells at the Mirabelle and Criterion restaurants working for the celebrated Marco Pierre White.

In 2001, he joined the team at The Square, a two Michelin-starred restaurant in Mayfair, West London. Working under Phil Howard, a chef who had a profound influence on his career, Brian became aware of the importance of the provenance of food – meeting the growers and producers, of knowing and understanding suppliers, and of sourcing and using the very best seasonal ingredients. This remains integral to his cooking ethos today. In turn, he has become a mentor to many of Belfast's young, up-and-coming third wave chefs.

He spent a year travelling the world soaking up the food cultures and cooking techniques in Australia, Asia and Mexico. He returned to Northern Ireland in 2003 to help head up the team at Shanks restaurant in County Down under the late Robbie Millar, where he worked for two years. He then joined the team at Shu on the Lisburn Road in 2004 and raised the culinary bar in Belfast. A clutch of awards, proudly displayed in the restaurant's hallway, reads like a roll call of excellence spanning over a decade. Brian was named Ulster Tatler's Chef of the Year 2011 and appeared on BBC Two's Great British Menu the same year. But not one to rest on his laurels, he is driven to expand his culinary boundaries. Despite his vast experience, he still enthusiastically travels to London for staging – an unpaid internship in another top chef's kitchen to learn new techniques and cuisines. The term originates from the French stagiaire meaning trainee or apprentice. The experience keeps him fresh and helps him to stay ahead of the curve on new food trends. It's just one of the reasons why Shu scooped the Best Restaurant in Northern Ireland title for the third year in a row at the 2014 National Restaurant Awards and is listed in the Top 100 Restaurants in the UK.

In recent years, just cooking food has not been enough for Brian. Inspired by his long-standing symbiotic relationships with local growers and producers, he has taken it back to basics. To relax, he grows and produces accent ingredients in his garden at home to enhance his famously flavourful dishes. It helps him connect with the genuine nature of seasonality and has fuelled a new respect for the authenticity of ingredients. He now regularly augments his restaurant dishes with produce from his garden – clearly something from which he draws great satisfaction. It's a down-to-earth approach that keeps him directly in touch with the land and demonstrates his total commitment to his craft.

Like Brian himself, Shu's modern Irish menu is uncomplicated and unpretentious. His food is bursting with life and vibrancy. On his À La Carte menu, dishes include Clandeboye Wild Pigeon, Lentils, Glazed Chicory and Pomegranate Molasses or Rare Breed Jacob Lamb, Wild Garlic Gnocchi, Peas and Shiitake Marmalade. But it's the alchemy of location, menu, interior design and knowledgeable staff that gives Shu its distinctive identity. Brian provides the inspiration and energy behind all those essential elements. He is unafraid to demonstrate he really loves being a chef. He consistently delivers exciting, quality dishes in a welcoming environment making Shu a Belfast institution and a destination restaurant for locals and tourists alike.

shu

ENGLISH ASPARAGUS, SMOKED ALMONDS, SHIITAKE AND MISO DRESSING

Serves 4

Core Ingredients
16 English asparagus spears
50g smoked almonds, chopped
300g fresh shiitake,
    stalks removed

Miso Dressing
1 tbsp soy sauce
2 tbsp mirin
1 tbsp miso paste
2 tsp grated ginger

Method
1. For the Miso Dressing, mix the soy, mirin, miso paste and ginger until the miso has dissolved, stir in two tablespoons of warm water. **2.** Bring 200ml of water to the boil in a medium pan. Slice half the shiitake and dice the other half. Add to the boiling water, give a good stir for 20 seconds, drain. Leave for 30 seconds. Place into a bowl and mix in the miso dressing. **3.** Cover with cling wrap and leave to marinate, stirring again after 10 minutes. **4.** Heat a non-stick pan over a medium heat. **5.** Snap the ends of asparagus and season, placing in the pan with some oil. **6.** Lightly colour each side (about 1½ minutes), remove and keep warm. Do in two batches if needed.

Assembly
Mix the asparagus and mushroom dressing together with smoked almonds and some salad leaves. Divide onto four plates.

Shu

SEARED HAND DIVED STRANGFORD LOUGH SCALLOPS, WILD GARLIC GNOCCHI, CELTIC MUSTARD

Serves 6

Core Ingredients

6 large hand dived scallops,
    removed from their shell
    and cleaned – ask your
    fishmonger to do this for
    you, sliced in half
lemon

Wild Garlic Gnocchi

3 King Edward potatoes
    (200g when cooked)
6 wild garlic leaves, sliced
33g oo flour
salt
1 egg
50g extra virgin olive oil
25g Parmesan

Dulse Dressing

100ml water
40g dulse

Celtic Mustard

8g cumin seeds
    (toasted and ground)
400ml vegetable oil
1 tsp Dijon mustard
1 egg
100ml water for dressing

Method

1. To make the Gnocchi, preheat oven to 180°C. Take the potatoes and prick them all over with a fork, put them on a tray lined with salt, place into the oven and bake for approximately 1 hour or until cooked through. Once the potatoes are baked, remove them from the oven and allow to cool slightly.
2. Cut the potatoes in half and push through a drum sieve into a large bowl. Add the flour and eggs to the bowl along with the wild garlic and season well. Work the mixture into a thick dough with your hands. Just bring the mixture together, do not knead as this will make the gnocchi tough. **3.** Divide the dough into two pieces and roll one piece into a long sausage about 2cm thick. Once you have your sausage, use a large knife to cut it into 2cm slices – they should look like little pillows. Put these formed gnocchi onto a lightly floured baking sheet until required. Repeat. **4.** Blanch the gnocchi in boiling water then refresh in iced water. When cool, drain and place onto a cloth. Place in the fridge until needed (this can be done a few hours earlier).
5. When ready, heat a non-stick pan, season gnocchi and fry each side for 1 minute or until hot. Remove from pan and add Parmesan on top. Keep warm.

6. Blanch garlic leaf and place on the side of each plate. **7.** Heat a non-stick pan until really hot, season scallops on both sides with salt and pepper. Add a splash of oil then add scallops and cook for 2 minutes each side (according to size), add lemon, remove and keep warm. **8.** For the Dulse Dressing, mix the water and dulse together. **9.** For the Celtic Mustard, place egg in a beaker and blitz in all ingredients except oil. Then add oil slowly. Add lemon if needed.

Assembly

Serve as shown.

Shu

VALRHONA CHOCOLATE TART SLICE

Serves 6

Base
40g sugar
50g ground almonds
30g cocoa powder
15g coffee
1g salt
25g butter

Topping
60g glucose
60g sugar
60g water
100g Valrhona 70%
100g Valrhona 55%
250ml semi-whipped
    double cream

Passion Fruit Caramel
82g sugar
250ml passion fruit juice

Banana Ice Cream
250ml milk
105ml double cream
250g banana purée
1 vanilla pod
125g egg yolks
50g caster sugar

Method

1. For the Base for the chocolate tart, mix all ingredients in mixer. Bake at 160°C for 20 minutes. Remove and cool. Add 175g melted butter, mix and press into mould evenly. Place in the fridge. **2.** For the Topping, boil the glucose, sugar and water – do not reduce or it will split the chocolate. Add to chocolate in an electric mixer and mix at a low speed until the mix is cold. Fold in semi-whipped cream. Add to the mould. Set for 4 hours in fridge and slice. **3.** For the Passion Fruit Caramel, caramelise the sugar then add passion fruit and reduce by half. **4.** For the Banana Ice Cream, pour milk and cream into a saucepan. Slice the vanilla pod in half lengthways and scrape the sticky black vanilla seeds into the pan with the point of a knife. Drop the scraped pod in too, then bring the mixture almost to the boil. Turn off the heat just before it boils. Leave for 30 minutes or so, for the vanilla to flavour the milk. **5.** Beat egg yolks and 50g caster sugar until light in colour. Pour milk mix through a sieve onto the egg yolks and sugar, stirring until you get a thin custard. Pour it into a clean saucepan.

6. Warm the custard over a moderate heat and, stirring almost continuously with a wooden spoon, bring it slowly towards the boil. Once the custard is thick enough to thinly coat the back of a wooden spoon, remove it from the heat, add the banana purée, pour it into a cold basin and leave to cool. Once cool, refrigerate for at least 30 minutes before pouring into an ice cream machine and churning until almost frozen.

Assembly
Serve as shown.

Shu

TEDFORDS KITCHEN

ALAN FOSTER

TEDFORDS KITCHEN: ALAN FOSTER

Occupying a highly desirable waterfront site, Tedfords Kitchen, owned by Chef Alan Foster, is one of the newest additions to Belfast's thriving restaurant scene. Historically, Lanyon Quay has been a barometer of the city's changing moods and fortunes. When shipbuilding ceased at Harland and Wolff, the area suffered a period of neglect. But in 1997, the lights started to come back on when the Waterfront Hall opened. This world-class entertainment and conference venue became the cultural beating heart of regeneration. The entire area slowly began to be reclaimed by businesses, restaurants, tourists and city natives. Two decades later, it has become one of the most attractive and iconic areas in the city.

While the tentative steps of regeneration were being taken on Belfast's waterfront, Chef Alan Foster was ably wrestling the Celtic Tiger himself in the kitchen of Dublin's quayside Clarence Hotel. Owned by U2's frontman Bono and guitarist The Edge, it was famed for its luxury and was a favourite bolthole for international celebrities. It was certainly a long way from the farm in Castlewellan, Co. Down, where Alan grew up. But his early experiences helping prepare meals for an army of seasonal workers who would descend on the farm each year instilled a passion in Alan for cooking which would see him become one of Belfast's most respected chefs.

As a young man, he aspired to become either a chef or an architect. His future path was set when he went to catering college and then in 1990 to work at the four-star Burrendale Hotel, nestled beneath the Mourne Mountains. The hotel's reputation for quality inspired Alan to work hard and master the techniques of classic French cuisine. He perfected the art of creating soups, stocks and sauces from scratch and realised the importance of using good quality, fresh ingredients. The hearty rabbit stews served with farm fresh potatoes and vegetables of his childhood were a good grounding in the rounded flavours still evident in his food today. He worked his way up to the position of Head Chef in the hotel and then moved to work in The Clarence's kitchen for a year at the height of its popularity.

Then he fell in love – twice. Firstly, with his wife Sharon, also his long-term business partner and the person he credits with his success, and secondly with a tall, empty, narrow building facing the waterfront area. Built in 1843, Tedfords was a former ship chandlers perfectly positioned to serve its target customers. In 2001, he took a leap of faith and in that characterful building he opened a quality seafood restaurant catering to the tastes of the slowly flourishing business and arts community populating the area. Tedfords quickly gained a great reputation for excellent, fresh local seafood served in an opulent interior, reminiscent of a luxury cruise liner.

Like Alan himself, Tedfords is solid, consistent and discrete. That's what his many loyal patrons love. It's also what's kept the restaurant an award-winning city favourite for over 15 years. Scrumptious fusion dishes like Curry Roast Monkfish with Coconut Rice, Pak Choi and Shellfish Wonton are legendary and remain on the menu by popular demand while changing seasonal specials showcase the best of fresh, homegrown produce.

For 15 very successful years, Alan watched the waterfront area flourish and grow outside his front window. And when the time was right in July 2015, he and Sharon launched a new venture, Tedfords Kitchen, across the road at Lanyon Quay. This youthful addition to his stable shares its more mature sibling's ethos of serving exceptional food but in a much more casual way. Offering all day casual dining on its riverside terrace or airy interior dining space, at lunch you can pop in for a Duck Hotdog served on a Brioche Bun or wait until the neon sign fizzes on at dusk and indulge in Braised Rabbit Spring Rolls, Apple Slaw with Sweet and Sour Peppers from the dinner menu. In keeping with the location's maritime heritage, Alan Foster has turned his mainsail to the wind and looks set to continue surprising and inspiring his patrons and peers with innovative, world-class food.

SCALLOPS AND WHITE PUDDING

Serves 4

Core Ingredients
8 large scallops
4 slices pancetta
4 shallots, cut in half
8 asparagus spears
sea salt

White Pudding
190g oatmeal
200g water
300g minced pork shoulder
1 onion, finely diced
10g salt
2g white pepper
2g ground ginger
2g allspice
2g nutmeg
2g mace

Confit Yolks
4 egg yolks
150ml olive oil

Wild Garlic Purée
2 shallots
1 garlic clove
40g butter
250g wild garlic
small bunch of tarragon
    and chervil
50ml double cream

Onion Purée
4 onions, finely sliced
30g butter
1 tsp sherry vinegar
2 tsp sweet soy sauce

Method
1. For the White Pudding, tip the oatmeal into a large bowl and soak in water for 1 hour, mix in remaining ingredients and roll mixture into sausages 2cm thick, wrap in cling film, simmer in a saucepan of warm water for 20 minutes then cool in iced water.
2. For the Wild Garlic Purée, melt butter in saucepan and sauté shallots and garlic over a moderate heat until soft and translucent. Add garlic leaves, tarragon and chervil and cook for a few minutes, purée with double cream until smooth.
3. For the Onion Purée, set the halved shallots onto a tray and roast in a hot oven (180°C) for 10 minutes until soft. Fry onions in butter until caramelised, purée with soy sauce and vinegar, pass through fine sieve then fill the shallots and keep warm.
4. For the Confit Yolks, pour olive oil into a small roasting dish, submerge egg yolks in the oil and gently cook in an oven at 65°C for 50 minutes, set aside until ready to serve.

Assembly
Place the pancetta on an oven tray and cook until crisp. Cook the asparagus in boiling salted water until tender, refresh in iced water. Slice white pudding into 1cm thick pieces, brush scallops and white pudding with oil, season with sea salt and then cook in a hot pan for around 1 minute on each side. Warm asparagus in the same pan as scallops. Arrange the crisp white pudding, scallops and asparagus onto a warm plate along with filled shallots, pancetta and set a yolk on top of white pudding. Pipe wild garlic purée onto the plate and drizzle with rapeseed oil.

Tedfords Kitchen

CURRIED ROAST MONKFISH

Serves 4

Red Pepper Purée
a little olive oil
1 onion, finely diced
2 red peppers,
    skinned and diced

Curry Oil
1 onion, finely diced
2 tbsp curry powder
100ml rapeseed oil

Coconut Rice
300g jasmine rice
170ml coconut milk
170ml water
salt and pepper

Pak Choi
2 tsp sesame oil
2 heads pak choi
4 tbsp soy sauce
1 lime, juiced

Monkfish
4 monkfish fillets
    (120–150g each)
4 tbsp curry powder
30g plain flour
1 teaspoon salt
2 tbsp oil for frying

To Serve
chopped coriander leaves

Method

1. For the Red Pepper Purée, gently fry onion and red peppers in oil until tender, season, purée and pass through a fine sieve. **2.** For the Curry Oil, sauté diced onion and curry powder in a little rapeseed oil until soft and then pour in the remaining oil. Cook gently for 2 minutes, pass through a fine sieve and discard the onions. **3.** For the Coconut Rice, simmer jasmine rice in coconut milk and water for 20 minutes until tender. **4.** For the Pak Choi, wash and trim the pak choi, heat a little of the sesame oil in a hot pan or wok and stir fry for a few minutes, add remaining oil, soy sauce and lime juice and cook for another few minutes. **5.** For the Monkfish, mix the curry powder, flour and salt together, add the pieces of monkfish and coat well in the seasoned flour. Heat the oil in a large frying pan and cook fish on both sides until golden. Remove from pan, place onto a roasting tray and cook at 180°C until a skewer can be pushed through with little resistance.

Assembly

Spoon coconut rice onto a serving plate and set the curried monkfish on top. Pipe red pepper purée onto the plate and drizzle with curry oil. Arrange pak choi and drizzle with soy and lime sauce, sprinkle with coriander and serve.

RICE KRISPIE BUN, CHOCOLATE PANNA COTTA, SHORTBREAD, CARAMEL AND SALT CARAMEL ICE CREAM

Serves 4

Chocolate Panna Cotta
250ml double cream
150ml milk
75g dark chocolate
150g sugar
1½ gelatine leaves, soaked
    in cold water until soft,
    then squeezed dry

Hard Caramel
75g butter
35ml cream
75g sugar
25g glucose
pinch salt

Shortbread
260g flour
¼ tbsp salt
225g butter (softened)
60g icing sugar

Rice Krispie Bun
60g rice krispies
60g dark chocolate
30g white chocolate

Salt Caramel Ice Cream
275ml cream
275ml milk
2 egg yolks
125g sugar

Soft Caramel
113g butter
120g cream
3 tbsp water
60g glucose
200g sugar

Raspberry Purée
150g fresh raspberries
30g icing sugar

Method

1. For the Chocolate Panna Cotta, boil cream, milk and sugar in a saucepan. Remove from heat and stir in chocolate and softened gelatine. Pass through a fine sieve and pour into moulds. Refrigerate until set. **2.** For the Hard Caramel, boil cream with butter, add sugar, glucose and salt, continuously stirring with spatula, until a dark caramel. Thinly spread onto a silicone mat and cool. **3.** For the Shortbread, cream butter and sugar together until light and fluffy. Add flour and salt and mix until a dough forms. Roll out to 5mm thick. Cut into twelve 2cm × 5cm rectangular pieces. Refrigerate for 20 minutes before baking at 180°C for 15–20 minutes until pale golden brown. **4.** For the Rice Krispie Buns, melt the chocolate together and stir in rice krispies. **5.** For the Salt Caramel Ice Cream, boil milk and cream. Whisk egg yolks and sugar together. Pour half the hot cream onto the eggs and sugar while whisking, return to pan and gently cook for 1 or 2 minutes, stirring all the time until it will coat the back of a wooden spoon. Pass through a fine sieve before churning in ice cream machine until frozen, store in a freezer.

6. For the Soft Caramel, boil sugar, water and glucose, use a sugar thermometer and cook until 151°C, then remove from heat. Pour melted butter and cream into hot sugar and stir. Line a small tray with oiled greaseproof paper, pour caramel into tray and refrigerate until set before cutting into small diamond shapes. **7.** For the Raspberry Purée, blitz raspberries and sugar in a blender and pass through a fine sieve to remove seeds.

Assembly

Remove the panna cotta from its mould and place onto a serving plate. Layer the rice krispie mixture in between three shortbread pieces and decorate with caramel diamonds and raspberry purée, set onto plate with a scoop of ice cream and a caramel shard.

THE
BARKING
DOG

MICHAEL O'CONNOR

THE BARKING DOG: MICHAEL O'CONNOR

For the last eight years, West Belfast-born Michael O'Connor has been the man behind the menu of The Barking Dog, one of the city's more eclectic eateries. Located in the University Quarter, Michael and his quirky restaurant have built up a large following of loyal patrons who come back time and again for his innovative, flavourful dishes served in a warm, relaxed and welcoming atmosphere.

Having trained in his youth under the famously fearsome Chef Marco Pierre White, Michael takes a pugilistic approach to his cooking, serving flavours that always pack a big punch.

It was under White's intense tutelage, in the white heat of his Michelin-starred Mirabelle in London's Mayfair, Michael learned advanced preparation techniques and the importance of putting in the effort to make sure ingredients fulfil their taste potential.

This training gave him an excellent grounding in classic French cuisine and the confidence to develop his own personal style – clearly the keys to his popular menus of today.

After a stint at a local catering college and initial training at the Balmoral Hotel in Belfast, Michael moved to London in 1997, gaining experience in some of the city's finest gastro pubs. He worked in the renowned Chelsea and Fulham gastro pubs The Admiral Codrington and The Salisbury Tavern, favourite haunts of the rich and famous who demand the highest standards of food served in a relaxed atmosphere.

Michael further expanded his skills and hospitality repertoire in Australia, where he took up the challenge of establishing the flagship restaurant of an elite casino overlooking Sydney Harbour that had just undergone a multi-million-pound refurbishment. Michael's solid grounding in classic French cuisine and his rounded under-standing of the hospitality industry helped the Astra Restaurant in Star City Casino secure a Chef's Hat, the Australian equivalent of a Michelin star, in just a year. He returned to the UK to take the helm for two years of another historic award-winning pub, The Gun in London's Docklands, named London's Best Gastro Pub by Time Out Magazine.

With every step on his career journey, Michael has absorbed a range of diverse skills and knowledge that he now combines in his own unique, unpretentious style. On returning to Belfast in 2008, Michael knew he wanted to create a restaurant that is the culmination of his life's experiences. Consequently, The Barking Dog is the outward manifestation of Michael's culinary ethos and lifelong food passions. His early food inspiration comes from big family Sunday gatherings when his Granny Annie would dish up meaty soups and casseroles, lovingly bubbled on the stove all day. These hearty homespun feasts were always followed by generous wedges of glistening apple pie served on a mishmash of heirloom crockery.

It's no surprise then these cherished food memories appear on his current menu in luscious modern incarnations.

He has unashamedly taken the food he loves to eat and re-imagined it in a distinct new way but still evoking his past by proudly serving his food on characterful mismatched plates. His award-winning signature dish, The Barking Dog Beef Shin Burger with Rocket, Caramelised Onions, Tomato, Cheddar and Horseradish Mayonnaise, takes three days bubbling, marinating and reducing to create a taste experience like no other. His Apple Tarte Tatin with Vanilla Ice Cream and Caramel Sauce is simple but exquisite.

Michael has created a beguiling bistro that consistently outstrips all expectations. The menu is big on flavour while the atmosphere is relaxed and unpretentious. There's a warming familiarity in his perennial favourites. Their comforting presence on the menu encourages diners to experiment with his more adventurous offerings. Michael prides himself on providing something to suit all tastes. His recipe for success is serving top-notch food based on the best locally-sourced ingredients in a warm and welcoming environment at an accessible price.

STEAK TARTARE

Serves 4

Core Ingredients
240g fillet steak, diced
4 tsp shallots, diced
4 tsp gherkins, finely chopped
4 tsp capers, finely chopped
8 tsp tomato ketchup
1⅓ tsp Dijon mustard
8 dashes Tabasco sauce
8 dashes Worcestershire sauce
4 small quail eggs
salt and pepper
chopped soft herbs

Method
1. Add all ingredients to a mixing bowl leaving the quail egg to the side and mix really well. Season to taste. **2.** Form the tartare in a ring mould using the back of a spoon pressing a small indentation in the middle to set the egg yolk in.
3. Separate egg yolk from the white and place on top of the tartare.

Assembly
Serve with crostini or crusty bread.

The Barking Dog

BEEF SHIN BURGER

Serves 4

Core Ingredients
1kg beef shin on bone
1 small onion
1 small carrot
1 small leek
1 head garlic
2 sticks celery
4 sprigs thyme
2 bay leaves
1 bottle red wine
10 white peppercorns

Stock
2 litres beef stock
1 litre chicken stock

Burger Patty
500g lean beef mince
1 small onion, finely chopped
2 cloves garlic, finely chopped
10 sprigs thyme, picked
¼ bunch flat leaf
    parsley, chopped
50g tomato ketchup
25g Dijon mustard
1 small handful breadcrumbs
1 small egg

Caramelised Onions
3 large onions, peeled and sliced
30g unsalted butter
30g Demerara sugar

Horseradish Mayonnaise
100g good quality mayonnaise
2−3 spoons horseradish
    cream to suit

Method
1. Marinate the 10 core ingredients for 24 hours. Drain off the liquid and reserve. Sear the meat in a hot pan with no salt and colour the vegetables. Meanwhile, reduce the liquor by half. Place into a deep roasting tray and cover with beef and chicken stock. Cover in tin foil and cook in preheated oven at 110°C for 10−12 hours. **2.** When the meat is fully cooked and tender, pass the contents through a colander with a bowl underneath to preserve the cooking liquor. Reduce the liquor in a large pot until you have a demi glaze. Pick the meat off the bone and shred. Add demi glaze to the meat and mix well. Leave to cool for 10−15 minutes and roll into a sausage inside cling film. Wrap in tin foil and 'Christmas Cracker' it. Leave to hang in fridge for 12 hours. **3.** For the Burger Patty, sweat onions, garlic and thyme off in a pan with some olive oil and leave to cool. Mix all ingredients together combining well and season. To construct the burger, using a metal ring take 6oz of burger patty and 2oz of beef shin and form the burger shape. Leave to rest for 2−3 hours to allow to set. **4.** To cook the burgers take a non-stick frying pan and heat well. Add some extra virgin olive oil and seal both sides of the burger, until golden brown. Place into a preheated oven at 200°C and cook for 12−14 minutes for medium. Turn halfway through to evenly cook.

5. For the Caramelised Onions, put the butter and onions into a heavy-based pot. Cook the onions in butter until the onions begin to colour and the water from the onions has all but evaporated. Add the sugar and cook further until onions are golden brown and the sugar has been fully cooked out.

Assembly
Serve with caramelised onion, horseradish mayonnaise, cheddar cheese, sourdough bun, rocket and tomato.

The Barking Dog

APPLE TARTE TATIN

Serves 4

Core Ingredients
4 apples, peeled and cored
100g butter
100g sugar
2 cinnamon sticks
100g puff pastry

Method
1. In a non-stick frying pan, add diced butter, sugar and cinnamon. Cut the apples in half, place flat side down and cover with a disc of puff pastry cut to slightly larger than the pan. Tuck the excess in the edges of the pan. Leave to rest for 1 hour in a fridge. **2.** Caramelise the sugar and butter on a low heat until golden brown and then bake in the oven at 180°C for 18–20 minutes until pastry is golden brown.

Assembly
Turn out on to a plate (upside down), dust with icing sugar and serve with your choice of ice cream.

The Barking Dog

THE GINGER BISTRO

SIMON McCANCE

THE GINGER BISTRO: SIMON McCANCE

It's appropriate that Chef Simon McCance's quirky restaurant The Ginger Bistro is located on Hope Street in Belfast. The address perfectly reflects its welcoming interior and sunny disposition. The well-worn mahogany floor, Moroccan-inspired lighting and fresh flowers on neat tables create an atmosphere of warmth at all times of the day. It's been a firm favourite with locals and tourists alike since it opened in 2004. Its quality offerings have been recognised with a string of awards including the Bridgestone and Michelin Guide, and it was previously named Best Restaurant in Northern Ireland in Which? Good Food Guide.

From the tender age of 12, Simon McCance loved cooking and wanted to own a restaurant. Originally from Lisburn, as a teenager he worked in a chip shop, burger bar and local hotels and restaurants, but he got his break aged 17 when he was offered a job in a restaurant called The Wallace in his hometown. In a small frenetic kitchen, he absorbed knowledge from the Head Chef like a sponge. They were tough lessons, hard learned. From prepping whole fish to butchering a variety of meats, Simon learned his cooking skills from the inside out. It gave him a forensic knowledge of the best way to prep and cook different cuts to maximise taste and value.

For a treat, his mother took him to the legendary Nick's Warehouse in Belfast for his 21st birthday. Over that meal, he vowed one day he would work in the kitchen at Nick's – one of Belfast's most popular and innovative restaurants in the '90s. As fate would have it, three weeks later he was prepping his own version of Asian Noodle Salad in the very kitchen he promised his mum he would work in. By the age of 25, he was Head Chef of Nick's Warehouse. Here began a lifelong friendship with multi-award winning Chef Nick Price and his wife, Cathy. Nick is universally recognised as one of the first wave of innovative chefs in Belfast to offer high-quality food in relaxed, casual surroundings. A favourite of the business community at lunchtime, and buzzing with bright young things in the evening, Nick's Warehouse represented the tentative green shoots of Belfast's culinary renaissance pushing hopefully up through the burning embers of a still conflicted city.

At 27, Simon took a career break and went travelling in Asia and Australia, absorbing new knowledge, cooking techniques and exotic flavours from the different food cultures he encountered. On returning to Belfast, with the help of Nick and Cathy Price, he set up the first incarnation of The Ginger Bistro on a micro-budget on the Ormeau Road. It quickly built a reputation for stunning food served at reasonable prices and a cult following of Belfast foodies beat a path to his door.

At the height of 'wee' Ginger's success, Simon was dealt a cruel and unexpected blow when he took seriously ill and was forced to close after two very fruitful years.

But with an inner reserve of determination and the motivation to succeed for the sake of his newborn twin boys, Simon fought his way back to health, took his chance and, close to Belfast city centre, opened the new The Ginger Bistro in 2004. Consistently serving Irish classics with a contemporary twist, in the last 12 years The Ginger Bistro has expanded physically to meet customer demand without losing any of its homely charms. A thoughtful, balanced, evolving menu reflects seasonal availability with in-demand favourites like Simon's famous Squid and Dips (Garlic Mayo, Sweet Chilli and Pickled Ginger) remaining on constant rotation for over a decade.

The spice ginger is renowned for its warmth and healing properties. It's both gentle and distinct. Subtle but determined. Simon McCance chose both the perfect name and address for this gem of a restaurant that so reflects his personality and his culinary journey.

ZINGY BEEF WITH A SALAD OF WATERCRESS, MINT, MANGO AND PEANUTS

Serves 1

Core Ingredients
4oz sirloin steak, trimmed
1 tsp olive oil
salt
black pepper

Dressing
1 garlic clove
a piece of pickled ginger
fresh chopped chilli to taste
1 dessertspoon light soy sauce
juice and zest 1 lime

Salad
handful of watercress
2 scallions
5–6 mint leaves
¼ mango, peeled and sliced

To Serve
10–20 peanuts

Method
1. For the Dressing, chop garlic, pickled ginger and chilli, mix together with lime zest to form a paste. Stir in soy and lime juice.
2. To make the Salad, mix watercress, scallions, mint and mango in a large bowl. **3.** Lightly oil the steak and season. Cook in a very hot pan or barbecue to your liking, rest before carving into slices.

Assembly
Dress the salad, add beef and mix together. Arrange on a serving plate and sprinkle with peanuts.

The Ginger Bistro

ROAST FILLET OF HAKE WITH CLAMS, CHORIZO, FENNEL AND CANNELLINI BEANS, BLACK PUDDING AND PARSLEY

Serves 1

Core Ingredients

4oz hake
3 clams
1 tsp chorizo, chopped
small slice black pudding
small bunch parsley
½ garlic clove
1 tsp butter
olive oil
salt
pepper
5–6 green beans

Beans

½ fennel bulb
¼ onion
½ garlic clove
splash white wine
¼ pint chicken stock
cream
60g cooked cannellini beans

Method

1. For the Beans, finely slice the fennel, onion and garlic and gently fry until soft, add a splash of white wine and allow to evaporate. **2.** Add chicken stock and simmer until it has reduced by half, now add a splash of cream and further reduce until the sauce will coat the back of a spoon. **3.** Season as desired, add cannellini beans and reserve until later. **4.** In a small pan, crumb the black pudding and gently fry until crisp. **5.** Chop parsley and mix with garlic to make a paste then add a drizzle of olive oil to loosen. **6.** Blanch and refresh the green beans. **7.** Heat a non-stick frying pan, place hake skin side down and fry until golden. **8.** At the same time, place the clams and chorizo in a small saucepan and steam until the clams open. **9.** Gently warm the beans and fennel while the hake finishes cooking.

Assembly

Spoon beans and fennel onto a serving plate, place hake on top, add cooked clams, sprinkle with warmed green beans and black pudding crumb. Drizzle with parsley oil and serve.

The Ginger Bistro

LEMON CREAM WITH PUMPKIN SEED FLAPJACK, RASPBERRY AND MERINGUE

Serves 4

Pumpkin Seed Flapjacks
125g porridge oats
50g pumpkin seeds
75g butter
30g soft brown sugar
1½ tbsp golden syrup

Meringues
2 large egg whites
4oz caster sugar

Lemon Cream
250ml double cream
juice and zest 1 lemon
caster sugar to taste
½ sheet soaked gelatine

Raspberry Sauce
75g raspberries

To Serve
75g raspberries
fresh mint
pumpkin seeds

Method
1. To make the Pumpkin Seed Flapjacks, place porridge oats and pumpkin seeds into a mixing bowl. Melt butter, sugar and golden syrup in a small saucepan and stir into the dry ingredients. 2. Spread the mixture onto a biscuit tray and bake at 180°C for about 20 minutes until golden. Remove from the oven, cool for 5 minutes then cut into biscuits and allow to cool completely. 3. Meanwhile make the meringues and meringue shards. Whisk egg whites to soft peaks, add caster sugar and continue to whisk until stiff peak stage. 4. Line two small trays with greaseproof paper, use ¾ of the mixture and drop small spoonfuls of meringue onto the tray, thinly spread the remaining mixture onto the second tray and bake at 100°C for 1 hour until dry and crisp. 5. For the Lemon Cream, pour the cream into a small saucepan and bring to the boil, reduce the temperature and simmer for 1 minute. 6. Add caster sugar, lemon juice and zest, then continue to simmer for a further 30 seconds. Add softened gelatine to the cream and sieve into a dish then refrigerate until set. 7. For the Raspberry Sauce, blend raspberries and push through a fine sieve to remove the seeds.

Assembly
To serve, drizzle raspberry sauce on to a plate, top with spoonfuls of lemon cream. Crumble the flapjack and sprinkle over the top. Finish with meringue, raspberries, mint and pumpkin seeds.

The Ginger Bistro

THE
MERCHANT
HOTEL

JOHN PAUL LEAKE

THE MERCHANT HOTEL: JOHN PAUL LEAKE

There was a distinct air of anticipation in Belfast when, in 2006, the iconic five-star Merchant Hotel arrived. This opulent hotel is the glorious manifestation of the ambitious dream of hospitality entrepreneur Bill Wolsey. Through his considerable vision and investment, a magnificent landmark building, built in 1860 with architecture in Italianate, neo-classical style, has been re-established back at the centre of Belfast life. Its creation gave the city a real confidence boost regarding its tourism, hotel and restaurant trade. It is evident that Bill Wolsey sought inspiration from the world's greatest and most luxurious hotels, carefully tailoring The Merchant Hotel to the particular tastes of its location. His benchmark was, and remains, absolute excellence in atmosphere, design and, of course, dining.

The Great Room Restaurant delivers elegant, contemporary incarnations of classical dishes, all presented with impeccable service. Confidently located under the jaw-droppingly beautiful domed ceiling of the former Ulster Bank headquarters, The Great Room Restaurant is integral to the overall story of the hotel, but it is also special enough to have its own identity. As in its previous mercantile incarnation, it bustles with activity from dawn to dusk.

During the day, the enamelled glass roof diffuses the room with a soft, warm light as diners enjoy a relaxed breakfast, before the now iconic afternoon tea and lunch service begins. In the evenings, the lighting is dimmed, and the crimson velvet upholstery and gilded fittings conjure an intimate and romantic atmosphere in which to enjoy the quintessential fine dining experience.

When you eat beneath the cherub-adorned architecture of heaven, you expect the food of angels, and that's where Head Chef John Paul Leake enters The Merchant Hotel's contemporary story. Belfast-born John Paul knew he wanted to be a chef from the tender age of 11 when, during an exchange visit to Belgium, he had a culinary awakening. Transfixed by watching the process of the host family's grandmother preparing a rabbit dish, he had an epiphany as he realised the velvety textures and deep flavours achievable from well-prepared food made from the best fresh ingredients. To this day he says he can still recall the flavours of that meal.

Work experience in local restaurants followed at aged 16. John Paul was hooked on the excitement of a professional kitchen – it felt like home and the frenetic environment well-suited his inquisitive and energetic personality. He worked in a few established restaurants in Belfast for five years before travelling in Australia and South East Asia.

He then relocated to London to further enhance his culinary skills. He worked at the Michelin-starred Mirabelle restaurant for Marco Pierre White for over two years before joining the world-renowned two Michelin-starred restaurant, The Square. His next move was to Orrery before returning to Belfast in 2010. Appointed Head Chef of The Merchant Hotel, he now uses his world-class experience to showcase the best local produce on The Great Room's impressive and seasonally reactive menu.

John Paul's approach is earthy and authentic. He loves detail and precision. His culinary presentations are as classically fine in their architecture as the room in which they are served. But his food is so much more than a static work of art: it's a delicate but dynamic marriage of taste and texture created from the finest fresh local ingredients. His vibrant flavours are underpinned by lovingly-intricate preparation while retaining the ingredients' authentic origins. He embraces a 'farm to fork' philosophy to ensure the provenance, freshness and quality of his core ingredients. John Paul sets very high personal standards – it's what drives him to continually challenge himself to exceed the expectations of The Merchant Hotel's discerning patrons. His passion and commitment to excellence are deliciously conspicuous in all of his impressive dishes.

DRESSED KILKEEL CRAB, CUCUMBER JELLY, PRAWN BEIGNET, SOFT EGG, AVOCADO PURÉE AND WATERCRESS

Serves 8

Core Ingredients
3 medium crabs,
    approximately 800g each
1 lemon
100g chives, chopped
30g flat leaf parsley, chopped
3g cayenne pepper
3g celery salt
100ml mayonnaise
quail eggs

Avocado Purée
4 ripe avocados (flesh only)
100g crème fraiche
1 lemon, juiced
pinch salt
little cold water
    (to slightly loosen)

Cucumber Jelly
3 medium cucumbers,
    chopped
10ml sherry vinegar
pinch salt
2½g soaked gelatine
    for every 100g
    of cucumber juice

Prawn Beignet
50g self-raising flour
pinch salt
90ml sparkling water
2g lemon juice

Method
1. To cook the crab, fill a deep pot with water and bring to the boil. Place the crabs inside and cook for 16 minutes on a medium heat. Once cooked, place into the fridge until cold then take out and remove the legs, pick out the white meat and place into a medium bowl.
2. Zest the lemon into the crab and add the cayenne pepper, celery salt, herbs and mayonnaise. Mix very well then taste the mixture and add extra seasoning to taste. **3.** For the Avocado Purée, place all ingredients into the blender and blend until very smooth. If consistency is a little thick, loosen with the water then pass through an extra fine sieve.
4. For the Cucumber Jelly, blend the cucumbers with a pinch of salt and sherry vinegar until smooth, then add the gelatine and pass through an extra fine sieve into a 3cm deep tray. Leave to set in the fridge for 4 hours then cut into small square pieces. **5.** Boil the quail eggs for 2½ minutes then place into iced water. **6.** For the Prawn Beignet, mix all ingredients together and leave to set for 30 minutes. Lightly flour the prawns and deep fry until golden.

Assembly
Place crab mixture into round moulds and top with chives. Peel and serve eggs by cutting in half and sprinkling with a little cracked white pepper (caviar optional). This dish can be served with picked watercress, sour dough Melba, dill pickled cucumber and caviar.

The Merchant Hotel

SHORT SADDLE OF KERRY HILL LAMB, GOAT'S CHEESE COURGETTE FLOWER, BRAISED LAMB RAVIOLI, SMOKED AUBERGINE AND BLACK GARLIC

Serves 8

Core Ingredients

1 whole lamb short saddle
(ask butcher to bone
with belly on)
chicken stock
shallots, diced

Pasta Mixture

275g 00 flour
3 egg yolks
2 whole eggs
little olive oil

Goat's Cheese Courgette Flower

200g St Tola goat's cheese
zest 1 lemon
15g flat leaf parsley, chopped

Artichoke Purée

300g Jerusalem
artichokes, peeled
700g single cream
200g unsalted butter

Smoked Aubergine Purée

2 large aubergines
4 shallots, finely diced
pinch cumin
salt to taste
50g extra virgin olive oil

Black Garlic Purée

2 bulbs black garlic, peeled
4 cloves black garlic to garnish
100ml Madeira
200ml chicken stock
50g butter

Method

1. Cover lamb bellies with chicken stock and place into the oven. Cook at 150°C for 1 hour 45 minutes. Keep lamb in stock and leave at room temperature for 30 minutes. Drain stock, then pick lamb into small pieces and add diced shallots. Mix well until incorporated, add a little of the cooking stock, then form mixture into 15g balls and set aside until pasta is ready. **2.** For the pasta, blend flour for 10 seconds in food processor then add all of the eggs and olive oil. Place into a bowl, cover with cling film and place in the fridge for approximately 2 hours. **3.** Remove from fridge and roll out using the pasta machine until thin then cut into circular shapes using a fluted edge cutter. Place each 15g ball between two sheets of cut pasta, sealing the edges with a little cold water. **4.** To cook, place the ravioli in boiling water for 6 minutes, then serve. **5.** For the Courgette Flower, mix all ingredients in a bowl then place into a piping bag. Open up the courgette flower and remove the contents, then pipe in the goat's cheese and wrap in cling film. Slice the courgette stem twice longways, as this will help the flower cook through. **6.** To cook, place the courgette stem into the boiling water with the flower tied to a wooden spoon balanced over the pot for 3 minutes so the stem cooks partially. The flower will steam a little to soften the goat's cheese.

7. For the Artichoke Purée, dice up 600g of artichokes into medium pieces then place into a pot with the butter. Cook for 8 minutes. Add the cream and cook slowly until soft then blend until really smooth. **8.** For the Aubergine Purée, place the aubergines directly onto a medium open flame, consistently turning until the aubergine is coloured all the way around with a dark finish. When cooked, remove the skin and place the flesh into a blender with the cumin and shallots. Blend until smooth then add the olive oil and season. To serve, heat up in a small pan on a low heat. **9.** For the Garlic Purée, place the garlic into a medium pot with a tablespoon of reduced Madeira, then add the chicken stock. Cook very slowly for 10 minutes, then add the butter and blend in a food processor until smooth before passing through an extra fine sieve and serving at room temperature. **10.** For the Short Saddle of Kerry Hill Lamb, pan fry until golden then place into a preheated oven at 185°C. Insert a temperature probe and cook until 44°C, then take out and rest for 5 minutes before serving.

Assembly

When plating the dish place small pieces of black garlic on for extra texture and flavour. A thin crisp aubergine can also be added.

PASSION FRUIT TART, MANGO SORBET AND WHITE CHOCOLATE POWDER

Serves 10

Tart Case
272g cold butter
100g icing sugar
2 eggs
425g T55 flour
cooking beans

Passion Fruit Mixture
150ml cream
105g caster sugar
6 eggs
165g passion fruit purée

Passion Fruit Jelly
6 fresh passion fruit
50ml passion fruit purée
7½g gelatine (soak in cold
    water to soften)

Mango Sorbet
1 litre mango purée
800g stock syrup

White Chocolate Powder
100g white chocolate
300g maltodextrin

Method

1. Mix butter and icing sugar together then add eggs. Mix well then add the flour until you achieve a smooth consistency, then refrigerate for 2 hours. **2.** After the sweet paste is rested, roll out to 40cm round and place into a 26cm width by 3cm depth cake tin and leave for 10 minutes in the fridge. Line with cling film then place cooking beans inside and blind bake for 15 minutes at 175°C. Take out the cling film and beans, and make small fork marks in the pastry base and bake for a further 10 minutes or until golden in colour. **3.** Whisk one egg and brush the pastry case lightly with a pastry brush and cook for a further 5 minutes before removing from the oven and leaving to cool for 30 minutes before placing mixture inside. **4.** For the Passion Fruit Mixture, whisk all ingredients together and rest for 1 hour in the fridge. **5.** When making the tart, skim off the light bubbles on top if any, then place into the cooked tart cases and cook at 110°C for 30 minutes until set. Once cooked, leave at room temperature for 1 hour then pour on the passion fruit jelly (just enough to cover the top of the tart so the seeds are evenly distributed) then place into the fridge for 4 hours before taking out and cutting. **6.** For the Passion Fruit Jelly, place the purée and fresh passion fruit into a pan, heat up over a medium heat then add the gelatine. Mix until melted, cool slightly then pour over the ready-made tart.

7. For the Mango Sorbet, put the mango and stock syrup into a pot and bring to the boil. Place into the fridge until cool then churn in an ice cream machine until glossy consistency. Serve or keep frozen. **8.** For the White Chocolate Powder, blitz the maltodextrin in the blender on medium speed, add melted white chocolate in a steady stream, then blitz on high speed for ten seconds. Ingredients should come together to form a powder and is ready to serve.

Assembly
To serve the dessert, place some hazelnut crumble for texture alongside violet flowers and mango purée.

The Merchant Hotel

THE
MUDDLERS
CLUB

GARETH McCAUGHEY

THE MUDDLERS CLUB: GARETH McCAUGHEY

An elegant graffiti art statement on the outside wall of Belfast's newest eatery, The Muddlers Club, reads 'Know No Fear'. Parked beside it is a black Harley-Davidson watched over by the monochrome street art of a giant Masonic-inspired all-seeing eye directly opposite the bistro's front windows. These symbols, intentionally or accidentally, conflate to announce you are entering the darkly seductive culinary territory of Chef Gareth McCaughey.

Hidden in an alleyway off the cobbled backstreets of Belfast's historic Cathedral Quarter, The Muddlers Club is named after a secret society of rebellious United Irishmen who met undercover in the area in 1798 to hatch plans for political disruption. It's also a nod to the creatively daring, modern cocktails drawing patrons there now. The location is unapologetically discreet. The reflective burnished gold of the open kitchen wall pulls in amber light from the red Belfast brick outside conjuring a warm, ever-changing ambient interior hue. The tables are fashioned from reclaimed floorboards salvaged from old city buildings. Wall-length, folding doors push back to allow diners and cocktail sippers to spill uproariously out into the impromptu courtyard on balmy summer evenings. Gareth's dining is experiential and it extends beyond his impressive bistro's physical walls. All of this is metaphorical of Gareth's personality and cooking ethos – challenging, direct and immersive.

Growing up in Donghamore, Co. Tyrone, Gareth rejected the constraints of his rural upbringing. At age 18 he headed to London to The People's Palace in Southwark, training as a pastry chef for four years. After a year as Pastry Chef at Zandar at the Crowne Plaza Hotel, he returned to Belfast in 2001 to work at Ten Square's exclusive fine dining restaurant, Porcelain. He then joined Niall McKenna at the newly-opened James St. South where he worked for six years, striking up a close working relationship and friendship with colleague Chef Stephen Toman. His next step was as Head Chef at The Barking Dog where he developed his skills leading the kitchen and running the business end of things. In 2013, he reconnected with Stephen Toman as he was opening the now Michelin-starred OX on Belfast's Oxford Street. Here, he further honed his already impressive culinary skills, benefiting from ideas and techniques Stephen had learned working in France for the previous decade. But in a typically honest way, Gareth made no secret of the fact that he was determined to open his own place. For two years he grafted hard in the demanding kitchen at OX helping Stephen achieve his vision, while simultaneously making his lifelong dream a reality.

In August 2015, Gareth unveiled The Muddlers Club. With a menu based on meticulously prepared but simple dishes, a focused wine list and an extensive, exciting cocktail list, this modern bistro writes its own rules.

In an appropriately rebellious way, Gareth refuses to restrain his glorious food in a single restrictive category. He creates his menu specials inspired by the very best in-season, locally-sourced produce, delivered daily by a strong network of artisan suppliers he has built up relationships with over many years. While his dishes have all the lightness of modern European cooking, his flavours extol the rich, deep flavours that form the basis of classic French cuisine. His evening À La Carte menu features mouth-wateringly simple masterpieces like a starter of Scallops served with Jerusalem Artichoke and Speck or a main course of Salt-Aged Ribeye, Bone Marrow Gratin, Girolles and Smoked Chilli Butter completed by a dessert of Baked Rice Pudding with Lavender Ice Cream.

The Muddlers Club is not so hidden that a clutch of prestigious awards couldn't find it. Just eight months after opening it was judged Best Newcomer and Best Restaurant in Northern Ireland at the Irish Restaurant Awards and of course there's a waiting list to get a coveted table. Like its 18th-century secret society antecedent, The Muddlers Club has quickly built an excellent reputation through whispering between those in the know. Proof that if the food and ambience are good enough, people will actively seek it out. Its plaudits and popularity are a testament to Gareth McCaughey's raw talent and food genius.

SMOKED SEA TROUT, ROE, CHARGRILLED BROCCOLI, ALMOND AND CAESAR DRESSING

Serves 4

Core Ingredients

400g sea trout
a little olive oil
500g purple sprouting broccoli
100g flaked almonds (toasted)
100g quality trout roe
a small handful of borage,
    shiso, baby red chard
    and mustard frill

Smoke

100g oak wood chips
10g fleur de sel

Caesar Dressing

3 egg yolks
2 anchovies
1 garlic clove
3 dashes Worcestershire sauce
2 dashes Tabasco sauce
1 tsp Dijon mustard
1 tsp lemon juice
300ml vegetable oil

Method

1. For the Sea Trout, add the wood chips and salt to a smoker and heat until smoke appears. Brush the fish with a little oil and place into a smoker skin side down, seal the lid and smoke for 3 minutes. Transfer the trout to a hot oiled pan, skin side down and cook until pink in the middle. **2.** For the Caesar Dressing, place egg yolks, anchovies, garlic, Worcestershire, Tabasco, Dijon and lemon juice into a food processor and blend until smooth, slowly drizzle the oil into the processor until the dressing is thick and creamy. **3.** Cook the broccoli in boiling salted water for 2 minutes, remove, brush with oil and chargrill for a few minutes.

Assembly

Drizzle Caesar dressing onto a large plate, top with broccoli, flake the smoked trout onto the plate, sprinkle with roe, almonds and mixed leaves.

The Muddlers Club

SALT AGED RIBEYE, BONE MARROW GRATIN AND SMOKED CHILLI BUTTER

Serves 1

Steak

1 salt aged ribeye, on the
    bone aged for 28–35 days
    in a salt chamber
1 baby carrot
1 baby beetroot
1 rainbow carrot
30g girolle mushrooms
1 wild garlic leaf
1 spoonful of celeriac purée
    (recipe below)

Vegetable Stock

1 white onion
1 carrot
1 leek
1 clove garlic
½ lemon
2½ litres water

Celeriac Purée

1 celeriac
300ml vegetable stock
    (recipe above)
30g unsalted butter

Smoked Chilli Butter

1 shallot
1 clove garlic
50ml white wine
250g unsalted butter
100g smoked chipotle chillies
2 sprigs thyme
pinch salt and pepper

Bone Marrow Gratin

1 piece bone marrow, trimmed
50g breadcrumbs
30g Parmesan cheese
1g parsley, finely chopped
zest 1 lemon

Method

1. For the Vegetable Stock (for Celeriac Purée), add the ingredients to a saucepan, bring to the boil and then simmer gently for 15 minutes, pour through a fine sieve. **2.** For the Celeriac Purée, peel and roughly dice the celeriac, add to a saucepan with enough vegetable stock to cover. Bring to the boil and then simmer until soft. Drain the celeriac and transfer to a Thermomix® (90°C), add butter and blitz until smooth and pass through a fine sieve.

3. For the Smoked Chilli Butter, soak chillies in hot water until soft, then remove and reserve the liquid. Remove the butter from the fridge to soften. **4.** Finely dice shallots, garlic, chillies and sauté in a hot saucepan with a little oil. Stir in thyme leaves, white wine and reduce, then add the chilli liquid and further reduce until very thick. Pour into softened butter and mix thoroughly. Season with salt and pepper before rolling into a log, wrap in cling film and refrigerate until hard. **5.** For the Bone Marrow Gratin, place the bone marrow onto an oven tray and roast in a hot oven (200°C) for around 20 minutes. Remove from oven, top with breadcrumbs, Parmesan, parsley and lemon zest. Return to the oven for a further 5 minutes until crisp.

Assembly

Peel the carrot and beetroot and cook in a saucepan of boiling salted water until soft. Wash the girolle mushrooms at least three times before sautéing in a hot pan with butter, salt and pepper. Cook the ribeye steak on a hot chargrill for a few minutes on either side to your liking. Spoon celeriac purée onto a serving plate beside the steak. Heat the vegetables and arrange on top of the steak. Add the bone marrow, butter and serve.

The Muddlers Club

CHOCOLATE, CARAMEL AND ESPRESSO

Serves 4

Caramel Sauce
115g butter
250g caster sugar
150ml cream

Milk Sorbet
2 cups milk
1 cup skimmed milk powder
1 cup condensed milk
1 cup caster sugar
1½ cups of water

Espresso Ice Cream
275ml milk
275ml cream
1½ shots espresso
125g caster sugar
2 egg yolks

Chocolate Tuile
50g icing sugar
10g self-raising flour
5g cocoa powder
25ml orange juice
30g melted butter

Caramel Shard
40g butter
20ml cream
40g caster sugar
12g glucose

Chocolate Ganache
110g dark 55% chocolate
125ml cream
1 shot espresso

Method

1. For the Caramel Sauce, cook the butter and sugar together in a saucepan until golden brown. Slowly stir in cream, bring to the boil and then pass through a fine sieve.
2. For the Milk Sorbet, pour milk along with milk powder, condensed milk, caster sugar and water into a saucepan and bring to boiling point, remove from the heat and pass through a fine sieve. Cool completely before churning in an ice cream machine until frozen. Store in a freezer. **3.** For the Espresso Ice Cream, pour the milk, cream, coffee and 125g sugar into a saucepan and bring to the boil. Whisk remaining sugar with the egg yolks until very thick (sabayon). Pour the hot liquid onto the sabayon while you whisk, then return all the liquid to the saucepan and gently cook for 2 minutes until it has thickened and coats the back of a wooden spoon. Pass through a fine sieve immediately and cool before churning in an ice cream machine until frozen. Store in a freezer.
4. For the Chocolate Tuile, sieve icing sugar, flour and cocoa powder together and stir in orange juice with melted butter. Spread the paste as thinly as you can in small rounds onto an oven tray with a silicone mat and bake in a hot oven (170°C) for 8 minutes. Remove from the oven and cool completely.

5. For the Caramel Shard, place butter and cream into a saucepan and boil, add sugar and glucose and continue to cook until a thick caramel. Pour onto silicone paper and spread, place another sheet of silicone on top and use a rolling pin to roll the caramel as thinly as possible. Allow to cool and harden.
6. For the Chocolate Ganache, heat milk, pour over chopped chocolate and stir until silky smooth. Pour the ganache into moulds and refrigerate until set.

Assembly
Set the chocolate ganache in the centre of a serving plate. Use a small blow torch to very lightly melt the top, pipe caramel sauce on top of the ganache and on plate, sprinkle with a little grated chocolate. Add quenelles of milk sorbet and espresso ice cream. Place pieces of chocolate tuile and caramel shards on top and serve.

ZEN

EDDIE FUNG

ZEN: EDDIE FUNG

It's not unusual to see Eddie Fung happily sweeping the Belfast street outside his flagship restaurant Zen ahead of lunchtime service. Personal humility and a laser attention to detail are exactly what have made this restaurant entrepreneur such a celebrated success. The popular and well-respected businessman arrived in Northern Ireland 30 years ago from his native Hong Kong, with no real plans.

His first passion was, and surprisingly remains, civil engineering. He has approached all of his successful projects with a logical engineer's eye and an emotional, sharing heart. It's an undeniably winning combination that has seen him open 25 successful restaurants in both England and Northern Ireland over the last three decades. To force himself to improve his language skills and excel in his academic studies, he jumped at the opportunity to work in a small Chinese takeaway in rural Irvinestown, Co. Fermanagh, for an immersive cultural and linguistic experience. The job provided just enough money to live on, and he signed up for a local college course as a route to university. He grins with pride recalling that he made history by being the first Asian student at the Fermanagh college where he excelled and was presented to Queen Elizabeth after graduating top of his class.

While still planning to pursue a career in civil engineering, to make money to fund both himself and his wife through university and to support his application for citizenship, he opened a small takeaway in Glengormley, a few miles outside Belfast. With no formal training as a chef, he drew upon his family's cooking skills – his parents helped prepare vast community feasts to celebrate the traditional autumnal Moon and Dragon Boat Festivals. He had honed his craft in the formal hospitality industry after selling his tiny takeaway for a profit and becoming manager of the acclaimed Chinese restaurant, The Water Margin in Ballymena. Eddie used these experiences when he opened his first successful restaurant, The Red Panda, in Belfast in 1999.

By 2003, he had already built a reputation as a pioneering restaurateur. With an unusual clarity of vision and a 'can do' attitude, he invested significantly to transform a derelict red brick 19th-century mill in the centre of the city into Belfast's first Japanese fusion restaurant. In building Zen, he used his solid engineering skills and restaurant experience to bring his most inspiring concepts together to create one of the most impressive and glamorous restaurants in the city. Taking inspiration from London's Nobu and Hakkasan, this large bi-level space is fitted out with a dark, luxurious interior exuding Eastern promise and presided over by one of the largest Buddha statues in Ireland. Upstairs, a central 30-foot mirrored catwalk, flanked by glittering metal chains, leads diners down to intimate circular booths. Eddie has also brought in some of the best chefs in Asia to create a menu that elevates Zen's food to the sublime, while its famous cocktails conjure intoxicating flavours of the Orient. With evocative names like Kyoto Breeze, Golden Dragon or Osaka Lady, they are designed to both cleanse and tantalise the taste buds. Famous for authentic, freshly-made sushi and sashimi, Zen's dishes are a perfect fusion of locally-sourced and international ingredients. Signature dishes on its extensive menu include Sizzling General Tso Irish Fillet Steak with Cashew Nuts and Chilli or Fried Soft Shell Angry Crab with Red Chilli.

Eddie remains very hands on with the day-to-day running of both Zen and his new House of Zen restaurant, which opened in 2012 at Belfast's St Anne's Square. You are more likely to see him around the restaurant before the diners flood in with a toolbox in hand rather than a laptop, as he remains an engineer at heart who loves to physically build and improve. By definition, Zen means achieving enlightenment through meditation. It is clear Eddie has carefully considered and thought about every aspect of this gorgeous restaurant, dedicated to personalised hospitality and presenting the finest Asian cuisine. His contribution to the Belfast food landscape has been immense, setting new standards in Asian fusion cuisine that has yet to be matched or surpassed.

聖な花とされ

ナム・ハノイ。年に2〜3

に包まれる街。そこにはそ

たという幻の蓮華をはじめ、

ホテルも似合っていた。

GRILLED EEL MAKI ROLLS DRESSED WITH SMOKEY MIRIN SAUCE

Serves 1

Core Ingredients
10 inch piece fresh eel
5ml cooking wine
1 strip Japanese omelette
    (recipe below)
15g avocado,
    peeled and sliced
15g cucumber, finely sliced
120g cooked sushi rice
1 nori seaweed wrapping sheet

Japanese Omelette
2 eggs
½ tsp white sugar
½ tsp mirin
    (Japanese sweet wine)
¼ tsp soy sauce
¼ tsp vegetable oil

Smokey Mirin Sauce
90ml soy sauce
50ml mirin
50ml cooking sake
35g maltose
45g brown sugar
125g white sugar
25ml fish stock

Method

1. For the Japanese omelette, whisk eggs, sugar, mirin and soy sauce in a bowl until the sugar has dissolved. **2.** Place a non-stick square Japanese omelette pan over medium heat and brush with vegetable oil. Pour a thin layer of egg mixture into the hot pan and swirl to coat. When the egg layer is firm on the bottom but still slightly liquid on top, lift about 2 inches of the edge of the omelette with a spatula and fold over the remaining egg layer, fold the omelette again until a flat rectangular shape. Cool before cutting into ½ inch strips. **3.** For the Smokey Mirin Sauce, add soy sauce, mirin, sake, maltose, brown sugar, white sugar and fish stock to a saucepan and boil, then reduce the temperature and simmer gently until the sauce has reduced to a sticky glaze. **4.** Fillet the eel to remove the bone and thread onto two bamboo skewers before setting into a steamer (this will avoid any curving while cooking). Add 5ml of cooking wine to a large saucepan of boiling water, set the steamer on top and cook the eel for 15 minutes. Remove from the steamer, brush with smokey mirin sauce and grill until golden brown and crisp.

5. For the Maki Rolls, put the bamboo mat on a flat surface and place seaweed wrapper on top. Spread sushi rice thinly over the seaweed and turn it over. Lay slices of avocado and cucumber on the seaweed and top with a strip of omelette. Use the bamboo mat to roll the sushi towards you as tightly as possible, forming a long roll up and cut into six equal pieces.

Assembly
Remove the skewers and cut the eel into strips, lay on top of maki rolls and brush with extra smokey mirin sauce before serving.

Zen

CRISPY AROMATIC DUCK
WITH RED GRAPEFRUIT, PINE NUT, LAMB LETTUCE SALAD
AND HOMEMADE DRESSING

Serves 2

Core Ingredients

¼ duck (200g breast and leg)
100g lamb's lettuce
10g pine nuts
10g red grapefruit pieces
10g pea shoots

Aromatic Duck

1½ litres water
2 bay leaves
3 dried chillies
1 inch piece ginger,
  roughly chopped
1 garlic clove
1 cinnamon stick
½ tsp Szechuan peppercorns
1 star anise
¼ tsp fennel seeds
1 small piece liquorice
1 tsp cardamon pods
2 tsp light soy sauce
2 tsp soy sauce
2 tsp cooking wine

Tempura Batter

50g cornflour
75g plain flour
5g baking powder
pinch salt
iced soda water
vegetable oil

Homemade Dressing

1 clove garlic, crushed
1 small piece ginger,
  peeled and grated
1 tsp fresh coriander,
  finely chopped
¼ roasted red pepper
½ roasted red chilli
pinch black pepper
1 tsp Mizkan Suehiro vineger
1 tsp soy sauce
1 tsp potato starch
2 tsp white sugar
1 tbsp olive oil
1 tsp water
2 tsp vegetable oil

Method

1. For the Aromatic Duck, pour 1½ litres of water with aromatic ingredients into a large saucepan and add the duck, making sure it is completely covered by liquid. Boil for about 20 minutes and then remove the saucepan from the heat completely and leave with the lid on for 1 hour. **2.** Remove the duck from the aromatic liquid and cool completely. **3.** For the Tempura Batter, mix cornflour, flour and baking powder together and gently stir in the iced soda water until the batter is of coating consistency. Dip the duck immediately into the batter and deep fry in hot oil until golden and crisp. **4.** For the Homemade Dressing, place all ingredients into a blender and blend until smooth.

Assembly

Arrange lamb's lettuce in a serving dish, sprinkle with pine nuts and red grapefruit pieces. Cut crispy duck breast into slices and the duck leg into pieces and arrange on top of the leaves, drizzle with homemade dressing and scatter a few pieces of crispy batter with pea shoots before serving.

Zen

ZEN SIGNATURE MONKFISH TAILS WITH GRAPEFRUIT AND TANG YANG SAUCE

Serves 1

Core Ingredients

200g fresh monkfish tails,
  skin and bone removed
50ml kimchi sauce, bought
  from Japanese supermarket
20g lotus root slice
20g enoki mushroom
10g red grapefruit,
  cut into tiny pieces
1 piece banana leaf
½ lime

Tang Yang Sauce

1 tbsp vegetable oil
¼ small onion,
  finely chopped
1 ½ garlic cloves, chopped
1 plum, cut in half
  and stone removed
30ml mirin
30ml kimchi sauce
25ml garlic chilli sauce
10ml cooking wine
20ml light soya sauce
10ml dark soya sauce
10ml sake
½ tsp sesame oil
30g sugar
20ml vinegar
20ml tomato ketchup
10ml brown sauce
10ml Worcestershire sauce

Batter

50g cornflour
75g plain flour
5g baking powder
pinch salt
iced soda water
vegetable oil

Method

1. Coat the monkfish tail in kimchi sauce and refrigerate overnight.
2. For the Tang Yang Sauce, heat vegetable oil in a saucepan, add chopped garlic and onion and stir for 2 minutes, add sugar and cook for a further 2 minutes before adding the rest of the ingredients, bring to the boil, reduce the temperature and simmer until the sauce thickens. **3.** For the Batter, mix cornflour, flour and baking powder together and gently stir in the iced soda water until the batter is of coating consistency. **4.** Dip the lotus root slice and enoki mushroom immediately into the batter and deep fry in hot oil until golden and crisp. **5.** For the Monkfish, cut the marinated monkfish into four pieces and fry in a hot pan with a little oil until cooked. **6.** Pour tang yang sauce into a wok or saucepan on high heat and bring to the boil for 20 seconds. Poach the cooked monkfish in the sauce for no more then 10 seconds.

Assembly

Lay a piece of green banana leaf onto the middle of a warm serving plate and set monkfish pieces coated in tang yang sauce on top, dress with crisp enoki mushroom and lotus root and finish with half a lime and a sprinkle of red grapefruit pieces.

Zen

INDEX

THE BIG FISH

The cover of this book features
one of Belfast's most loved and
iconic statues. The 32-foot Big Fish
was created in 1999 by Belfast-born
artist John Kindness in response
to a commission to celebrate the
regeneration of the Docklands and
River Lagan. The artist chose the
Atlantic Salmon as a symbol of
renewal as the fish were beginning
to return to our waters. It proudly
stands on Donegall Quay and its
siting is significant as it is the
location of the confluence of the
River Farset with the River Lagan.
Each scale of the fish is a tile
depicting some aspect of Belfast's
past. On closer inspection, the
ceramic fish reveals a complex
mosaic of the city's history. It has
become emblematic for the entire
regeneration of the city in the last
two decades and perfectly embodies
the ethos of Belfast's flourishing
food landscape and the personal
stories of the chefs and restaurateurs
who have worked so hard to put
the city on the international
culinary map.

We would like to thank
John Kindness for his full support
in featuring The Big Fish on the
cover of this book.

RESTAURANT CONTACT DETAILS

Coppi
St Anne's Square
Belfast, BT1 2LR
Phone: 028 9031 1959
www.coppi.co.uk

Deanes at Queens
1 College Gardens
Belfast, BT9 6BQ
Phone: 028 9038 2111
www.michaeldeane.co.uk/
deanes-at-queens

Deanes Eipic
28–40 Howard Street
Belfast, BT1 6PF
Phone: 028 9033 1134
www.deaneseipic.com

General Merchants
481 Upper Newtownards Road
Belfast, BT4 3LL
Phone: 028 9065 2708
www.generalmerchants.co.uk

Graze
402 Upper Newtownards Road
Belfast, BT4 3GE
Phone: 028 9065 8658
www.grazebelfast.weebly.com

Hadskis
33 Donegall Street
Belfast, BT1 2NB
Phone: 028 9032 5444
www.hadskis.co.uk

Home
22 Wellington Place
Belfast, BT1 6GE
Phone: 028 9023 4946
www.homebelfast.co.uk

Howard Street
56 Howard Street
Belfast, BT1 6PG
Phone: 028 9024 8362
www.howardstbelfast.com

James St. South
21 James Street South
Belfast, BT2 7GA
Phone: 028 9043 4310
www.jamesstreetsouth.co.uk

Mourne Seafood Bar
34–36 Bank Street
Belfast, BT1 1HL
Phone: 028 9024 8544
www.mourneseafood.com

Neill's Hill
229 Upper Newtownards Road
Belfast, BT4 3JF
Phone: 028 9065 0079
www.neillshill.com

OX
1 Oxford Street
Belfast, BT1 3LA
Phone: 028 9031 4121
www.oxbelfast.com

Saphyre
135 Lisburn Road
Belfast, BT9 7AG
Phone: 028 9068 8606
www.saphyrerestaurant.com

Shu
253 Lisburn Road
Belfast, BT9 7EN
Phone: 028 9038 1655
www.shu-restaurant.com

Tedfords Kitchen
1 Lanyon Quay
Oxford Street, Belfast, BT1 3LG
Phone: 028 9027 8823
www.tedfordskitchen.com

The Barking Dog
33–35 Malone Road
Belfast, BT9 6RU
Phone: 028 9066 1885
www.barkingdogbelfast.com

The Ginger Bistro
6–8 Hope Street
Belfast, BT12 5EE
Phone: 028 9024 4421
www.gingerbistro.com

The Merchant Hotel
16 Skipper Street
Belfast, BT1 2DZ
Phone: 028 9023 4888
www.themerchanthotel.com

The Muddlers Club
Warehouse Lane
Belfast, BT1 2DX
Phone: 028 9031 3199
www.themuddlersclubbelfast.com

Zen
55–59 Adelaide Street
Belfast, BT2 8FE
Phone 028 9023 2244
www.zenbelfast.co.uk

THANK YOU

The idea for this book has been brewing for some time now and with 2016 being Northern Ireland's Year of Food, it seemed a perfect time to get it out there.

With the decision made I knew the perfect team to produce the book was already in place.

Long time friend and journalist Joanna Braniff would write the book, my son Dean Pauley, a London-based graphic designer, would design the book and Cheryl and I would handle the photography. All we needed now was to convince the 20 chefs/restaurants we had drawn up on a list that this book was a fantastic idea.

Everyone on our list of 20 said yes and their enthusiasm and commitment was extraordinary. A lot of chefs arranged photography to take place on days the restaurants were closed, bringing in all their staff to make sure everything was in place to get the best results possible. Their attention to detail was amazing and their passion shone through in every plate of food presented to us to photograph. I can't thank the 20 chefs/restauranteurs enough as without them there wouldn't be a book and I hope they are as proud of it as I am.

Dean and Joanna's attitudes to their roles were equally as impressive as the chefs, with them revisiting every detail in a constant strive for perfection, thanks a million guys.

Our copy editor Alix Britton joined our little team along the way and has done such a fantastic job, thanks Alix for all your hard work.

Thanks to our friend Karyn Booth for helping out on a few technical issues, you came along at just the right time.

I also have to thank Andy Rea who was the first chef I spoke to about the book and his encouragement and help has been invaluable. Andy made a lot of introductory calls to the chefs and without those calls I still might be waiting for appointments.

A big thank you to my friend Andrew Campbell for his help in driving the project along and giving me so much helpful advice on producing the book.

I'd like to thank Paul Rankin for writing the foreword, so good of him to be part of this book as his contribution to the Belfast food scene has been immense.

Last but certainly not least I want to thank my partner and soul mate Cheryl Johnston.

So often the unsung hero of The Studio, Cheryl is the person who makes things happen and keeps the cogs turning, every task carried out with a smile on her face. I want to thank Cheryl not only for the huge contribution she has made in getting this book to print but also for being the most beautiful person to share my life with ... love always.

David Pauley

First published 2016 by
The Studio Publishing Company

Photography Copyright
David Pauley – The Studio

ISBN 978-1-5262-0471-4

Photography:
David Pauley – The Studio
www.thestudio-photography.com

Design:
Dean Pauley
www.deanpauley.co.uk

Written by:
Joanna Braniff
jo.writeherewritenow@gmail.com

Copy Editor:
Alix Britton
alix.britton@gmail.com

Production Manager:
Cheryl Johnston

Printed by:
W G Baird

Recipes supplied by
individual restaurants

The Studio Publishing Company
19C Weavers Court
Linfield Road
Belfast, BT12 5GH

www.belfastonaplate.com